TALES OF NATURAL AND UNNATURAL CATASTROPHES

ALSO BY
PATRICIA HIGHSMITH

NOVELS

Strangers on a Train
The Blunderer
The Talented Mr. Ripley
Deep Water
A Game for the Living
This Sweet Sickness
The Cry of the Owl
The Two Faces of January
The Glass Cell
A Suspension of Mercy
Those Who Walk Away
The Tremor of Forgery
Ripley Under Ground
A Dog's Ransom
Ripley's Game
Edith's Diary
The Boy Who Followed Ripley
People Who Knock on the Door
Found in the Street

SHORT STORIES

Eleven
The Animal-Lover's Book of Beastly Murder
Little Tales of Misogyny
Slowly, Slowly in the Wind
The Black House
Mermaids on the Golf Course

TALES OF NATURAL AND UNNATURAL CATASTROPHES

PATRICIA HIGHSMITH

THE ATLANTIC MONTHLY PRESS
NEW YORK
♦

First published in Great Britain in 1987 by Bloomsbury Publishing Ltd.
First Atlantic Monthly Press paperback edition, January 1990

Published simultaneously in Canada
Printed in the United States of America

Library of Congress Cataloging-in-Publication Data

Highsmith, Patricia, 1921–
    Tales of natural and unnatural catastrophes / by Patricia
Highsmith.—1st American pbk. ed.
    ISBN 0-87113-341-5
    I. Title.
PS3558.I366T35   1990   813'.54—dc20   89-15151

The Atlantic Monthly Press
19 Union Square West
New York, NY 10003

FIRST PRINTING

CONTENTS

The Mysterious Cemetery   9

Moby Dick II; or The Missile Whale   20

Operation Balsam; or Touch-Me-Not   34

Nabuti: Warm Welcome to a UN Committee   53

Sweet Freedom! And a Picnic on the White House Lawn   67

Trouble at the Jade Towers   82

Rent-a-Womb vs. the Mighty Right   107

No End in Sight   127

Sixtus VI, Pope of the Red Slipper   140

President Buck Jones Rallies and Waves the Flag   162

THE MYSTERIOUS CEMETERY

O n the outskirts of the small town of G— in eastern Austria lies a mysterious cemetery hardly an acre in size, filled with the remains of paupers for the most part, their places marked by nothing at all, or at best by tombstone fragments now all in the wrong spots. Yet the cemetery became famous for its odd excrescences, bulbous figurines of bluish-green and off-white colour, which eerily rose above the surface of the soil and grew, some, to a height of two metres or so. Others of these mushroom-like growths attained only fifty centimetres, some were even smaller, and all were bizarre, like nothing else in nature, even coral. When several such small ones had manifested themselves above the grassy and muddy earth, the cemetery caretaker called it to the attention of one of the nurses in the adjacent National Hospital. The cemetery lay to the rear of the red-brick hospital building, so one did not easily see the cemetery when approaching the hospital on the one road that went past it with a turn-off toward the hospital's front doors.

The caretaker, Andreas Silzer, explained that he had knocked down a couple of these growths with his hoe, taken them to the compost heap expecting them to rot, but they hadn't.

'Just a fungus, but there's more coming,' said Andreas. 'I've put fungicide down, but I don't want to kill off the flowers with anything stronger.' Andreas faithfully cared for pansies, rosebushes and the like which a few relatives of the deceased had planted. Occasionally he was tipped for his services.

The nurse did not answer for several seconds. 'I'll speak to Dr Müller. Thank you, Andreas.'

Nurse Susanne Richter did not report what Andreas had said. She had her reasons, or rationalisations. The first was that Andreas was probably exaggerating, and that he had seen a few big mush-rooms on the tombstones because of all the rain lately; secondly, she knew her place, which wasn't a bad one and she wanted to

9

keep it and not become known as a busybody meddling on territory not assigned to her, namely the cemetery.

Almost no one set foot in the dark field behind the National Hospital except Andreas, who was about sixty-five and lived with his wife in town. He bicycled to work three days a week. Andreas was semi-retired, and received a stipend for his cemetery and hospital ground-tending in addition to his state pension. The approximately three-a-month funerals were usually attended by the local priest who said a few words, by the gravediggers who stood by to do the filling in, and only about half the time by a member of the deceased's family. Some of the elderly men and women who died were quite alone in the world, or their children lived far away. It was a sad place, the National Hospital Number Thirty-six.

It was not sad, however, to a young medical student of the University of G— named Oktavian Ziegler. He was twenty-two, tall and thin, but possessed of an energy and sense of humour that made him popular with girls. He was also a brilliant student, and rather favoured by his teachers. Oktavian – he was so called because his father, an oboist, worshipped the music of Richard Strauss and had hoped his son might become a composer – had been invited, in fact, to be present at some experiments that doctors of the hospital and a couple of his doctor teachers were making on terminal cancer patients at the National Hospital. These experiments took place in a large room on the top storey of the hospital, where there were long tables, several sinks, and good lighting. Sanitary conditions were not of the essence, as on this floor the experiments were done on corpses, or else upon bits of cancerous tissue excised from a living patient or from a corpse before it was buried in the cemetery. The doctors were trying to learn more about causes and cures and the reasons for the growth of cancer once it got started. In that same year, scientists in America had discovered that a particular quirk in one gene was a stepping stone toward cancer, but the dread disease needed a second stepping stone to start the malignant cells forming. Carcinogenic agents was the blanket term for the elements which when introduced into guinea pigs or any organism might initiate cancer if the host organism had by nature the first stepping stone. So much was now common knowledge. The doctors and scientists at the National Hospital wanted to learn more, the rate and the reasons for growth, the response of the cancer when massive doses of carcinogens were injected into already cancerous tissue, experiments that could not easily be performed upon living humans, but could upon an organ or a lump of tissue being nourished independently by a blood supply from a small pump, for instance. There was no way of purifying an amount of blood save by recycling the blood through cleansers or by constant supplies of fresh blood, but none of the doctors wanted to carry on an experiment for weeks on end. What the doctors and Oktavian did observe in regard to a cancerous liver section (from a dead patient) was that the diseased tissue, having been given carcinogenic agents, continued to grow even after the blood supply was halted and drained off. The doctors did not think it of any purpose to try to find out how large it would become, though they kept some of it to look at under their microscopes in case it could yield any new information. The disposal of these finally unwanted remnants took place in the cellar of the hospital where there was a good-sized furnace, separate from the heating system and used exclusively for the burning of bandages and soiled material of all kinds.

This was not so with the approximately three-a-month corpses which were buried without embalming and sometimes in a shroud instead of a wooden coffin in the cemetery. In some cancerous patients in their last days, when morphine had dulled their senses and local anaesthesia could do the rest, doctors injected carcino-genic agents, hoping for an explosive breakthrough, as journalists might say, though the doctors never would have used such a term. The cancers did enlarge, the patients being terminal did die, and not always any sooner because of these tests. Sometimes the enlarged growths were excised, mostly not.

Oktavian was given the chore, considered a menial one suitable for a student, of seeing that the 'test corpses' got down by the big old back elevator from the top storey lab to the cemetery, after a brief stop in the basement morgue for coffin or shroud. The gravediggers were part-time workers with other jobs. Oktavian had to telephone the two or three of them, sometimes on short notice, and they all did the best they could. One of the men was usually a little drunk, but Oktavian stuck with it, joked with the men, and made sure the grave was deep enough. Sometimes they had to inter a corpse on top of or right beside another. Lime was sometimes put down. This of course was for the poorer dead, who had no relatives attending. It was on one of these inhumations in autumn that Oktavian noticed the rounded excrescences that Andreas had reported to the nurse just days before. Oktavian noticed them as he puffed a rare cigarette and stomped his feet against the cold. He knew at once what they were and what had caused them, and he said not a word to the shovelling workmen near him. He did investigate one (he saw at least ten) near him, tripping over a fallen tombstone as he went, as it was rather a dark night. The thing looked bluish-white, was about fifteen centimetres high, rounded at the top with what looked like a convolution or crease half way down it that disappeared in the earth. Oktavian was surprised, amused, anxious all at once. By comparison with what he and his seniors had produced in the lab, these growths were huge. And how big were they underneath the soil to have poked their way nearly two metres to the surface?

Oktavian returned to the gravediggers, and realised that he had been holding his breath. He supposed, he was almost sure, that the growths out there in the darkness were highly contaminous. They would combine the carcinogens injected by the doctors as well as the original berserk cells that had caused the cancer. How large would they become? And what was nourishing them? Terrifying questions! Oktavian, like most medical students, sent chums an odd part of the human anatomy once in a while. It was almost a token of affection when a fellow received such a present in the post from a girl student, but something like *this*? No.

'Let's tread it down!' Oktavian said to the labourers, setting an example by starting to stomp on the rise of earth that marked the new grave. *Stomp, stomp, stomp*, all four of them together. And how long would it be before a pale curve pushed through the soil, Oktavian wondered?

The young man saved his secret until the following Saturday night when he had a date with Marianne, the girl he had considered for about a month now his favourite girl.

Marianne wasn't very pretty, she studied like a demon, seldom took the time to put on lipstick and barely combed her light brown hair for their dates, but Oktavian adored her for her ability to laugh. After all her grinding away at her books, she could explode with joy and freedom after she closed the books, and Oktavian liked to think, though he was too realistic to believe it, that he was the sole agent of her transformation.

'Something special tonight,' Oktavian said when he picked her up in the downstairs hall of her dorm. He had asked her to wear galoshes, and she had. Oktavian had a two-seat motorcycle.

'You don't mean we're going hiking in the dark!'

'Wait!' Oktavian zoomed off.

It was raining slightly, there were gusts of cold wind. A wretched night, but it was Saturday night, Marianne clung to Oktavian's waist, ducked her helmeted head and laughed as Oktavian sped into the countryside.

'Here!' he said finally, stopping.

'The hospital?'

'No, the cemetery,' he whispered, and took her hand. 'Come with me.'

He held her hand all the way. The ghostly pale growths were higher, Oktavian thought, or was he imagining? Marianne was speechless with astonishment. She couldn't laugh. She gasped, puzzled. Oktavian explained to her what the growths were. He had brought a torch. One bulbous thing was nearly a metre high! It looked rather like a foetus, Marianne remarked, at that stage when fish and mammal show their rudimentary gills under the head-to-be. Marianne was artistic; Oktavian might never have remarked that.

'What're they going to *do*?' she whispered. 'Don't the doctors know about this?'

'I dunno,' Oktavian replied. 'Somebody'll report it.'

Oktavian had been trying to draw her toward the centre of the dark field. Beyond and to their left, the five-storey hospital building loomed, with half its windows illuminated. The top floor was alight. 'Just look at that!' cried Oktavian, his wandering torch having touched on something.

This was a double growth, rather like a pair of Siamese twins with joined hips, two separate heads, and with two arms that showed fingers – not five fingers on each hand, but something like a few fingers – at the ends of both arms. An accident, to be sure, but weird. Oktavian smiled crookedly, but could not laugh. Marianne tugged at him. 'Okay,' he said. 'I swear – I think I just saw one of 'em *grow*!'

Marianne led the way back to the motorcycle. It seemed amazing to Oktavian that no doctor or nurse had looked out and seen what was going on in that field. Comical to think of doctors, interns, nurses all so busy at their appointed tasks that they hadn't a few seconds to look out of a window or take a short walk!

Half an hour later, when Marianne and Oktavian sat in a little inn eating hot and spicy goulash, while a cheerful fire crackled in a hearth not far from them, they did laugh, albeit in nervous spasms.

'. . . *got* to tell Hans!' Oktavian said. 'He'll flip out!'

'And Marie-Luise. And *Jakob*!' Marianne grinned like her Saturday evening self.

'Better have a party. Soon. Because the time is short.' Oktavian spoke earnestly across the table.

Marianne knew what he meant. They made plans, drew up a list of a select twelve or so. It should be next Tuesday night, they decided. Next Saturday might be too late, the hospital might have discovered the state of the cemetery and done something about it.

'A ghost party,' said Marianne. 'We'll come in sheets – even if it's raining.'

Oktavian did not reply, as Marianne knew him well enough to know that he was in accord. He was thinking, could rainwater contribute to the growth of those insane tumours? Could the soil? After the supply of blood in the corpses had been exhausted, could the busy blood vessels that fed the cancers start capturing earthworms, maggots for their meagre nutrients? Did the capillaries even reach out for adjacent corpses? Whatever the answers to those questions, the fact was plain that the death of the host did not mean the end of the cancer.

There were some smirks, some cynical disbelief, when Oktavian and Marianne extended discreet verbal invitations to the Real Ghost Party Tuesday Night at the Cemetery of the National Hospital Number Thirty-six. Wear a sheet or bring one and turn up at a quarter to midnight were the instructions.

Again it rained slightly on Tuesday evening, though there had been two or three days without rain, and Oktavian had hoped that the good weather would hold. However, the *Schnürlregen* did not dampen the spirits of the dozen or more medical students who arrived at the cemetery more or less punctually, some on bicycles, as they had been warned not to make any noise, because nobody wanted the hospital staff descending upon them.

There were muted 'Ooohs!' and other exclamations when the sheeted students investigated the burial ground, though Oktavian had admonished everyone to keep silent. 'It's phoney! – Plastic balls! You so-and-so!' one girl whispered loudly to Oktavian.

'No! – *No*!' Oktavian whispered back.

'Wheest! My God, look at this!' cried a young man, trying to keep his voice low.

'Cancer patients? Holy Mother of God, Okky, what kind of experiments are going on here?' said an earnest fellow near Oktavian.

Sheeted figures circled the cemetery, drifted among the tombstones in the moonless night, shining pocket torches carefully downward to avoid tripping and detection. Oktavian had imagined calling for a circular ballet-of-ghosts round the cemetery, but was afraid to use his voice for this, and there was no need. Out of nervous excitement, fear, collective puzzlement, the students began a dance not at first in the same direction, but a dance which soon organised itself into a counter-clockwise ring which stumbled, recovered, held hands, hummed, giggled softly, and wafted its pale and sodden sheets in the wind.

The lights of the National Hospital glowed as ever, nearly half the windows bright rectangles of light, Oktavian noticed. He was holding Marianne's hand and that of another fellow.

'Look at this! Hey, *look*!' said a boy's voice. The boy was focusing his torch on something as high as his hip. '*Pink* below! I *swear!*'

'Shut your trap, for *Chris*' sake!' Oktavian whispered back.

At that moment, Oktavian saw a young man on the other side of the ring kick at a pale lump, and heard him laugh. 'They're fixed in the ground! They're *rubber!*'

Oktavian could have killed the fellow! He didn't deserve to get his medical degree! 'It's real, you fool,' Oktavian said. 'And *shut up!*'

'*Measles, magpies, maggots, mumps!*' the students chanted, swinging their legs as in a conga line. The circle slowly rotated.

A whistle blew.

'Okay, *run!*' Oktavian shouted, realising that a hospital guard had seen or heard them, maybe the old guy who was half the time asleep at midnight just inside the front doors. Oktavian ran with Marianne toward his motorcycle at the edge of the road.

The others followed, laughing, falling, crying out. Some had cars, but the cars were a little distance away.

'Hey!' Oktavian said to a boy and girl near him. 'Keep this *quiet*! Pass the word!'

They dispersed in surprisingly good silence, sheets folded, like a trained army. Oktavian rolled his motorcycle several metres before starting the motor. Behind them, slowly moving figures with torches, people from the hospital, were investigating the edges of the cemetery.

Oktavian lay low in the next days. He had plenty of work to do at the university, and so had the others. But they looked at the *G— Anzeiger*, the town newspaper. There was not even the tiniest item about a 'disturbance' or 'vandals' in the National Hospital's cemetery, and this silence Oktavian had foreseen: the authorities could not afford to report that anyone had trampled on the graves or upset a couple of flower pots, because then they would have some of the relatives of the deceased coming to rectify the damage and to complain about lack of care, and the hospital would not want the public to learn about the odd growths, numerous enough now to catch anyone's eye. The hospital people must be thoroughly alarmed, Oktavian thought.

On Thursday evening, Oktavian went to the National Hospital at 9 as usual to join the doctors on the top floor. He had glanced at the cemetery when he parked his motorcycle. The cemetery had been as dark as ever, but he had still seen pale balloon shapes in it, six or seven, maybe the same as before. Upstairs, the atmosphere was different. Dr Stefan Roeg, the youngest of the doctors and the one Oktavian had always got along best with, said hello and then good night in almost the same sentence. He had his overshoes and umbrella in his hands, though it wasn't raining, and plainly he had turned up just to collect them. Old Professor Braun, whose head was in the clouds and whose head was bald except for the long wisps of grey hair above his ears, was the only person among the seven of them who acted the same as ever. He was ready to talk about the 'progress' of little bits of tissue under glass bells since last week. Oktavian could see that the others had given it up. Their faces wore polite smiles as they bade Professor Braun good night.

'It is dangerous,' one doctor said hastily to Professor Braun before he departed.

Oktavian also managed to sneak out. Would old Professor Braun keep on working till after midnight, all alone? Oktavian and the doctors were silent as they tramped down the five flights of stairs. Oktavian thought it wise to ask no questions. They all knew an awful secret. The doctors were treating him, a mere student, as one of them. Had the doctors a plan of action? Or were they simply going to keep quiet?

Word somehow leaked out. A few curious townspeople went to peer from a distance at the cemetery, Oktavian noticed when he paid a quick visit on his motorcycle. The three or four people were not venturing into the cemetery, just standing and staring from its edges at the growths which resembled tied-down balloons in the dusk. It was ghosts; evil spirits from the criminals and the horribly ill who had been buried there; it was an outlandish result of fall-out from atomic bomb testing; it was because of insanitary conditions at the National Hospital, which everyone knew was not the most modern of the nation. Marianne reported some of these explanations to Oktavian, having heard them from her dormitory housekeepers who hadn't even seen the cemetery.

The death of Andreas Silzer was announced in the *G—Anzeiger* in a small paragraph. 'Faithful caretaker of the National Hospital grounds.' He had died of 'metastatic tumours'. Poor old Andreas would have been exposed for months to the growths in the cemetery, Oktavian thought. Were the authorities ever going to clean the place up?

Oktavian and Marianne rode up to the National Hospital one Saturday evening, and saw two large trucks in the parking area of the hospital. A couple of lanterns on the cemetery ground gave some illumination, and they saw figures moving about. On closer inspection, they could see that the figures wore surgical masks, grey uniforms, and wielded picks and shovels with gloved hands.

'Garbagemen!' Marianne whispered. 'Look! They're sticking the things into big plastic sacks!'

Oktavian saw. 'Then what do they do with the sacks?' he said almost to himself. 'Come on. Let's leave.'

Only two days later, a garbageman collapsed. His wife refused to let him be taken to the National Hospital, and said he had got sick from working in the cemetery. Her talking took the lid off, because her words were printed in the *Anzeiger*. At once the other 'sanitation workers' began complaining of nausea and weakness. The cemetery and a few metres beyond it were cordoned off by a heavy wire fence with danger-of-death signs attached at intervals. A wide gate in the fence permitted the entry of a bulldozer which tore up the ground. Disinfectants of all kinds were poured on to the soil by workmen wearing coveralls and masks. Patients and staff were evacuated from the National Hospital, and the building itself was washed and disinfected. The *Anzeiger* said that a strange fungus had attacked the cemetery, and that until the medical authorities learned more about it, it was deemed wise to close the grounds to the public.

But the growths kept coming, small low-lying curves at first, all over the cemetery's churned surface, then came faster growth as if out of nowhere – one metre, two metres in a fortnight. Artists came to sketch, sitting on campstools. Other people took snapshots, and the more wary stood at a distance and looked through binoculars. There was talk of massive removal of the cemetery's soil to a depth of two or even three metres. But where would the authorities dump it? The Preservation-of-the-Sea people had weeks ago pushed through legislation: the cemetery soil from National Hospital Thirty-six of G— was not to be dumped into ocean or sea. Farmers and ecologists of the country protested against the burial of the cemetery on their land or on public land at whatever depth. Border guards of adjacent countries were double-checking lorries going out of the country, lest they be concealing cemetery débris.

Incineration was therefore decided on. Danger money reached absurd heights for the men who worked with derricks, getting the soil into containers which were wheeled to the hospital's back door, through which so many corpses had moved in the opposite direction. The big old heating furnace and the waste furnace of the hospital were back in service, the only things in the building that were. The ashes came out to a smaller bulk than the soil, black and dark grey, but were handled by the workmen with similar caution. Were these to be dropped into the sea? No, that was forbidden too. There was really nothing to do with the ashes but store them in heavy plastic sacks in the basement morgue and on the ground floor of the building for the nonce.

And still the growths came, as if hundreds of spores had been scattered by all the hacking and digging, but that was merely a poetic thought, Oktavian reflected, because tumours did not grow from spores. Still it was amazing how fertile that cemetery soil was! But he forgot the National Hospital while he took his final examinations. Marianne had another year to go. Then they were thinking of marrying.

Despite some noisy official disapproval, but cheers from the radical-left-in-the-arts, sculptors began to include in their exhibitions works inspired by the forms they had seen and sketched in the National Hospital Thirty-six cemetery. These sculptures were not unpleasing, being composed of many curves like buttocks or breasts, depending on how one chose to interpret them. Some won prizes. One nearly-abstract resembled a plump woman holding a beach ball; another of a seated figure was called 'Maternity'.

The cemetery ground, though lower, continued to throw up its strange fruit. Masked and gloved workers – old pensioners mainly – hacked at their bases with hoes, as they might have hacked at stubborn weeds in their gardens at home. The roots of some growths were so deep that the workmen were inspired to suggest that the ground be excavated and burnt again. The town authorities were sick of it. They had already spent millions of schillings. They would simply keep the whole area fenced off and try to forget it. The road there didn't go anywhere except past the empty hospital and up into the mountains where it became a lane used mostly by hikers. The cemetery would be forgotten. The press had already fallen silent on the subject. It was known that doctors had been conducting experiments relating to cancer in the National Hospital, but the blame for the cemetery's condition was spread over so many, that no doctor or hospital administrator was charged with responsibility.

The authorities were wrong in thinking that the cemetery would be forgotten. It became a tourist attraction, surpassing by far the popularity of the Geburtshaus in G— of a minor poet. Postcards of the cemetery sold fantastically well. Artists came from many lands, scientists too (though their tests on specimens taken from the cemetery yielded no further information on the causes and cures of cancer). Artists and art critics commented that nature's designs, as manifested in the cemetery's growths, surpassed those of crystals in ingenuity and were not to be despised aesthetically. Some philosophers and poets compared the grotesque shapes to a man-made wreckage of his own soul, to an insane tinkering with nature, such as that which had resulted in the accursed atomic bomb. Other philosophers countered: 'Is cancer not natural to man?'

Oktavian remarked to Marianne that they were safe in asking such a question, because the answer could be yes and no, or yes or no to various people, and the talk about it could go on for ever.

MOBY DICK II; OR THE MISSILE WHALE

I t was the middle of the warm season, when the sun lay bright on the blue water, and the little fish swam near the surface. He cruised along near his mate, basking in the warming waters as she did, sounding sometimes for pleasure, rising to leap like a dolphin in full sunshine before crashing back into the soft sea. His mate was soon to have her pup, and she swam more slowly, nudging curiously into coves of islands. Both knew islands were dangerous, men lived on islands, but a mother whale likes to give birth in shallow water.

The South Pacific held not many ships where they were, and these few were long low things that kept a steady course. The little islands, so harmless looking, were more sinister, because of the catamarans and even canoes that sometimes set out after them, not to mention the occasional boat with a motor, sometimes equipped with a harpoon gun.

The whale and his mate had been together all their adult lives. This would be her second pup. The first, a female, having swum with them a long while, got lost a few times and been found again, thanks to the voices of the anxious parents, had in due time swum away on her own.

On one sunny afternoon, his mate turned toward a low-lying stretch of yellow land, and he followed at a distance. The water was not deep, and diving just a little way he could scrape the sand with his belly. Yellow-and-black-striped fish twitched and flitted out of his way with all the power in their tiny bodies. He might have captured several, strained the water out of his mouth, and enjoyed a titbit, but with a delicate wave of his tail he moved closer to the island and hung motionless in the water, listening for his mate. He heard a faint disturbance.

She was going to produce the pup at last.

A little column of water and air showed where she was, not far from the yellow beach with its palm trees tilting in the breeze.

'Hee-yoo!' cried a human voice.

Underwater he sounded a warning to her. He had heard human voices many times before, always different, yet always somehow the same. Under the water's surface, he saw her twisting, the pup half out. Now the men were pushing a boat into the water, and they yelped. He lifted his head and saw the first spear hurled.

She came floundering toward him, seeking deeper water. A spear projected from her back. He swam under and into the boat, catching it beneath its pointed front, and tossed it upside down. A spear struck him near his tail.

Now the men were in the shallow water, stumbling and swimming, they all had spears, and his mate was surrounded. The whale went forward and pinched a pair of men between his lips.

There were screams. Blood spread in the water.

A spear pricked his front and stayed there. Men were tugging his mate toward the shore. Others now turned their attention to him.

The whale flicked his tail with deliberate aim and a man flew into the air and burst, sending a shower of blood on to the sea's surface. He lunged with his mouth open: one little man and the lower limbs of another struck his underlip and were crushed a moment later. With a lift of his tongue, the whale rid himself of the bleeding human flesh and the sea water that accompanied them. His body stung from spears, and he swerved toward deeper water, raising his head for all the air he could get in a gasp, then he dived.

They were coming after him in a boat, not to be feared because it had no motor. He stung and hurt and he was furious. Far out from the island, he rose and spewed air and water, sighted the boat and dived again. When he saw the boat's slender form above him, he circled, then aimed himself at its side just below the surface, so the boat was crushed by his impact and also tipped over. The three or four yelling men in the water he bumped senseless, and left them.

Inspired by this, he headed again for the shore, where he knew his mate was dying or dead. Two more boats had put out, and he struck the nearer, rising under it, unseating the men and sending them into the water. The second boat hurled spears, one of which stuck in his side. He dived for safety, turned and sighted the boat which twisted above him, and rammed it. Then he moved on toward the shore, his belly near the sand. The shouts of the men grew sharper. Lifting his head, the whale saw with one eye the little brown men prancing around the half-beached form of his mate. The whale had an impulse to ram the lot of them, to swim right on to the beach, and just as suddenly the impulse was gone, he flicked his tail and swam away.

Encountering a large male shark, the whale lunged for him, just to see the shark scurry away, a flash of frightened white.

The odious little brown men! He was aware that the little beasts did not usually try to fight a creature the size of himself, or of his mate either. The little men attacked sea-cows a quarter his size. Sharks terrified them. The whale swam sullenly on, not caring about direction but unconsciously seeking cool streams for his wounds.

He was south of the equator and heading still south. He swam steadily till his anger abated a little and, when he came up for air, the sun was low on the horizon. Before dark, he met a vast school of small fish and swam into it with his mouth open.

In the next days and weeks he swam lazily, not having, at this time of year, any cause to head in any certain direction. The equatorial area of the Pacific was a huge world. And it was odd to be alone after five years of being with a mate, of knowing that she was somewhere near, able to be found soon, even if she was not in sight for a while. They had always refound each other, always agreeably gone in the same direction, usually one of his choosing.

He avoided the islands, though the little fish near their beaches were tasty, and so were the patches of green plants. Once in a careless moment he leapt a little and fell back, exhaling a tall jet of white steam, and his left eye saw a boat. The boat was distant, but it had the dark, thick shape of the ships that hunted whales, the kind of ship that had a motor. He had dived at once, without much air in him, and headed at a right angle away from the ship's course. Now it would be a matter of zigzagging, of trying to elude while still managing to get enough air to swim fast. Many a time he had evaded such vessels. Why not again? It was not a question, however, but a necessity.

The chase went on for half an hour, then one hour. The whale let the twisting, rocking ship come quite close, or rather close to his wake that he left after surfacing for air, then he sounded to swim under and astern of the little ship and to keep going.

For several minutes, the ship lost its quarry. Its motors at full speed made the ship keel hard as it turned, seeking, guessing.

He swam as long as he could before his exertions made him come up, and again he had to blow out before he took in air. The ship was now far away, but the whale knew he would have been seen. He inhaled for as long as he dared, then swam under the surface with a feint to the left, changing underwater to the same course he had been on before. Broad daylight, alas!

Two more hours passed. When again the ship was very near, the whale had not the strength for any great speed, and he was in need of air.

A harpoon gun cracked. The lance missed him, and its timed bomb exploded underwater at a distance of at least the whale's full length away from him. In crazy anger, he seized the metal cable of the harpoon in his mouth and tugged, as if he could upset the ship in this manner or even tow it. The thin cable was ridged, and cut his mouth a little.

The cable also cut the whale's huge but delicate tongue, and the man at the winch saw the blood on the water. They lowered a boat and idled their motor still more. The strong winch on deck began to pull the cable in.

The whale felt the tug of the cable in his mouth, heard the slap of a boat's bottom and knew what it meant: a boat with lances for the final strikes behind the fin, into the eye, down the spiracle, then ropes to fasten the corpse to the ship. Fools in their wooden boat!

With a slow gesture of his tail, the whale positioned himself to face where the slapping sound had come from. Now he could see the boat bottom. He rammed the little craft from below, rising with his back against it. At the same time, a lance hit him in front of his tail, across the end of his spine, stinging at once. The whale swam downward.

From the whaler ropes were flung to at least three men in the swirling water. The wooden craft had broken in half, ropes and lances had fallen into the sea. The screams did not stop: one man had somehow got his arm torn open on a jagged board and was bleeding badly, another floated face down and motionless, and a man from the ship went over the side with a rope to try to save him. The winch had dragged up an exploded but whaleless harpoon. And some others on the ship were surprised to see one half of the wooden boat floating away rapidly into the distance. The last lance hurled had lodged in the whale, and the end of the lance's rope was fastened to a metal ring in the boat's gunwale.

They could, of course, have followed the now visible whale track.

But the course of the whale was not their assigned course for one thing, and more than half the crew were occupied with the nearly drowned men and with recovering what they could of the lances and tackle of the other half of the boat before they abandoned it. But that crazy whale was a big one, they all agreed. Full of hell!

The whale by now realised that he had an appendage. The first time he had come up for air, he had not seen the hunk of wood behind him. The second time, he did. He had been aware of a resistance when he dived to a certain depth, though he was capable of pulling the half-boat underwater and of keeping it there, if he chose. The rope was flexible, not like the ridged cable, and was perhaps thrice his length. The boat fragment was irksome. It was wise to swim deep enough to keep the boat beneath the surface. Yet when he came up to breathe – and it took a long while and many inhalations to lay in a goodly store of air – the half-boat was going to float up behind him.

This fact caused some strange stories on the islands that the whale cruised past. Children and young boys told of a wrecked ship or boat which they had seen floating for a while, and which had suddenly disappeared. The story spread from island to island, repeated by the men and boys who encountered one another on their fishing boats, and was chuckled at yet not entirely disbelieved, because too many reliable men swore they had seen it.

'It is magic,' said one man, speaking in a respectful tone, because his people respected magic.

But was it good or bad? Might it mean good fortune or a catastrophe, like a great wind with a wave that would wash over their islands, flatten their houses, and send everyone into the sea? There were a few white men on some of the islands, and they professed to know about typhoons, earthquakes, eclipses of moon and sun. Maybe they did. But the appearing and vanishing boat was different. The white men would laugh at the story. But they didn't always know what was important and what was not. How could they? They were but men, after all.

Often when grazing on floating greenery or schools of tiny fish, the whale would lounge on the sea's surface, enjoying the warmth of the sun along his back. Usually there was no island within his vision, but the islands were no hazard, if he kept a distance. However, on one such lazy day when he nosed above the surface, he saw a catamaran with a sail making for him, or so it seemed. The suddenness and the silence of this approach stirred him with fear and defensiveness, and he dived a little and turned, so as to face the boat. The catamaran was the size of boat he could crack and seriously damage, if he so chose.

The whale perceived that the men were interested in the half-boat that floated to one side of him now. There were two men in the boat, and one had a rope in hand. The other man saw him, gave a shout, and quickly lifted a spear. The whale moved his horizontal tail and charged, gliding under the catamaran's projection, striking the side of the boat with his nose, staving it in. The standing man with the spear fell into the water, and the whale, having circled with a great churn of water behind him, bit the man's feet off. The other man was easier prey. The whale simply rammed his body, knocking the wind out of him and more.

The catamaran's mast with its sail wilted at a slant toward the sea. The whale might have lingered for another strike or two but, when he lifted his head for a quick breath, he heard the bark and shriek of men's voices, distant but clear. Another boat? The whale did not tarry, but dived at once, and swam away from the sounds.

The men were finished, one dead from crushed ribs and lungs, the other from loss of blood. A second catamaran had set out from the nearby island with the intention of rescuing the two men. They had not seen the whale, but they had seen the first catamaran break in half near the floating piece of boat, and then they had seen the boat piece disappear below the surface of the sea. So they approached the still-floating but broken catamaran with caution, and one of the men wanted to turn back while they still could.

'It is magic!' he said. 'You see? The boat is in two pieces and they are going to float and sink other boats now – and kill *us*!'

One man caught sight of a floating corpse. 'There is my *brother*!'

They had not expected corpses. They had expected to find the two men perhaps injured, but clinging to the wreckage of the catamaran. When a boy cried out that he saw the second corpse in a sea of blood, it was instantly and unanimously decided that they would turn back.

'Don't look at the boat!' yelled one man. 'Turn your eyes away!'

They turned their eyes away, the catamaran turned, paddles were plied until arms ached and the men gasped for breath. A man not rowing recited chants to ward off evil spirits. Back on the island, they told their story in frightened bursts, their knees shaking with a collective awe. The rest of that day and evening, the others on the island were afraid to touch any of the four men.

So that story spread, and was enlarged. The famous magically appearing and disappearing piece of boat had merely touched a catamaran and it had cracked in half! And the two men on board had been instantly killed as if struck by an evil spirit.

The half-boat was sighted off other islands and avoided. The possibility that the half-boat might be being towed by a shark or whale was actually uttered, but if so, it was the spirit of a whale or shark, impossible to kill, yet able to kill anything with ease, and to destroy any craft merely by its evil will.

The whale swam on in the temperate waters, irked less and less by the dull pain just above his tail, caused by the harpoon which passed into his coat of blubber and out, like a pin. The floating boat was the nuisance. The whale glided past rough underwater coral, thinking to wear the rope through or bump the boat from the rope, but so far he hadn't succeeded. He endured a sullen melancholy, all alone. He encountered three whales like himself, one a young female, the others males, and he might have joined them for company for a while, but one of the males shied at the boat that dragged behind him under the water. The whale was shunned.

So the whale sang alone in the deeps: 'Hoo-wa-a-aaah-ou' in a rather high-pitched tone, talking to himself. He used to communicate with his mate like that, telling her where he was, warning her of an enemy, or with another tone telling her that food was in sight where he was swimming.

One morning when he was floating hardly below the surface, bobbing up now and then to get an easy store of air, he heard the plash of a paddle.

The whale's left eye saw a tiny boat with a single figure in it, making not for him but for the wooden wreck which the whale knew floated to one side and behind him now. The little craft was no challenge, but the whale scanned the horizon for other boats, for an island, and saw a pale line of land quite a distance away. He swam a bit deeper.

The boy in the boat saw the whale, shuddered and half stood up, gripping his paddle in both hands. He had come out on a dare, and minutes ago he had said to himself, *I don't care if I live or die.* This had given him a crazy courage. He had imagined being struck dead by magic, by something he would not be able to see or understand.

Now he had seen, and that was a whale bigger than any he had ever heard about. He saw the shiny grey monster circling his boat just under the surface. His boat rocked wildly. The boy fell backwards, and without thinking shipped his long paddle for safety. The rope that held the half-boat to the whale glided past the prow of the boy's boat and touched it, making his boat turn. With his right hand the boy fended off the half-boat that might have damaged his canoe. The monster was still circling. The boy saw the long shining lance that passed through the whale's skin. It had a splendid point. It was made of metal, and was longer by far than the boy was tall. The boy coveted that spear. Could he capture it?

The madness that he had felt on his island returned: he did not care if he lived or died! As the rope slid by on the left side of his boat, the boy seized it just under the water. He felt the terrifying pull of the whale, and he took a tighter grip on the rope with both hands and set his teeth. What if the whale took him on a great voyage to the edge of the earth and down? What if the whale turned and swallowed him? The boy's boat moved, and he pitched forward, then got to his knees. His boat moved ever faster, first to one side then the other. Then suddenly the resistance was gone, and the boy fell backward, bare feet in the air for a moment. The rope hung limp in his hands, and he panted, scared, relieved and puzzled. He looked around but saw no whale, only a whirlpool in the sea nearby, where the whale had dived. He pulled the limp rope in hand over hand, and there was his prize – the beautiful lance!

The lance was even a little longer than his boat! It had an arrow-like tip, sharp and strong. At the other end, a metal ring, an integral part of the lance, served to hold the rope which was securely tied to it. The wreck of a half-boat floated near. The boy's parted lips began to smile. There was nothing to fear now. The lance was his, his weapon now. The half-boat, which his people had thought was magical, was nothing but part of a wreck. The whale had swum off. Or had it?

The boy gazed carefully around in a circle once, and then again. The waters looked calm. He took up his paddle, reached for the rope that lay over his boat's side, and gave the wreck a tug. There were valuable metal pieces on the wreck, he had noticed. He would burn these off and keep them.

On the beach of the island, the boy was erect and silent, like a chief of the old days. A crowd of his people had been waiting for him, had swum out to pull his boat and the wreck on to the shore. The boy answered their excited questions calmly and briefly, like a man. He carried the lance straight up beside him, and would not let anyone touch it at first, then he did – smiling proudly as older men ran their thumbs along its tapered edge. The girl he liked was watching from a distance. She did not take her eyes from him, but when he had set out on the desperate voyage to the wreck, she had said she did not want him. Now things would be different. The whole world was different for the boy.

It had occurred to the boy to say that he had killed the whale in whose body the lance had been fastened, but he decided against this. He simply told of a whale that had been pulling the half-boat, the biggest whale he had ever seen or heard of, as long as their island. He had managed to seize the end of the lance, he said, as the whale swam by, and had tugged it from the whale's flesh. This everyone believed. Everyone went and touched the wreck, as if to assure himself that it held no magic powers. Men lifted and let fall the metal ring that held the rope, listening to its clink against the metal in the wreck's side.

The boy was even haughty for a while toward the girl he liked, pretending not to see her, though she was the main thing on his mind. He said that the whale was not only huge but stuck all over with lances and harpoons like a big pig stuck with spices for roasting. The whale was so big, no weapon would ever penetrate to its vital organs. Thus the boy enhanced his courage.

That still left the whale, and the story of the impregnable monster became known in the islands, and lookouts were sharper on the little fishing boats, the idea being to avoid the beast. The story reached the ears of professional whalers, who with their harpoon guns were not afraid, and who reckoned that, even if the whale were not so large as reported, it would still be worth capturing. One of these whalers pursued the whale one day, and the whale eluded the ship by diving under and behind one of the long tankers that was moving on an undeviating course.

The whale was heading north into seas that were cooler now and would become still cooler. Enough of the islands! He had a few more bone-tipped lances in him since he had shed the boat fragment. A lance near his left eye annoyed him, especially when he swam past vegetation that the lance touched. He was in a rather irritable and fighting mood all the time. This caused him to cruise some distance up a river one day by mistake.

He had swum fast for several seconds into the river's broad estuary, not realising that it was not part of the sea, until the sour and bitter taste, the vibrations caused by something heavy being thrown in near him, alerted him to the fact that he was going in a wrong direction, toward a likely impasse as well as human enemies. He could even hear the churn of machinery. He turned and dived lower, heading back the way he had come.

The water was foul, the river bed covered with jagged metal pieces, cylinders large and small, rotting ropes and chains. Boats above him tossed in the disturbance he made on the river's surface, and men's voices cried out. The whale shot forward with a great thrust of his tail, and something scratchy swept over his head, tweaked a lance, and stuck.

For a few seconds he felt resistance, but not enough to stop him, and he reached the open sea at last. But when he paused, he felt a weight on either side of him, tending to pull him downward. He could see several weights on either side, all attached to one another on a cord which lay across the back of his head. The whale swam backwards, but the weights stayed with him. The rope or chain was somehow caught in the lances that stuck in him. He nosed toward one weight, but did not touch it: it was shaped like the floating things that bordered the routes into rivers, but these were smaller. To rise for air was now not so quickly done and, if he wished to cruise near the surface for brit, the weights came with him reluctantly, and slowly sank again.

On one of the whale's surfacings for air in the North Pacific, the sight of his high, white exhalation gave rise to a shout which the whale heard. He had come up rather close to a fishing boat, the kind with both sail and motor, the kind not to be feared. But the whale shot himself toward the boat for sport, to hear the men cry out again, and now their yelps sounded frightened. The whale realised that on either side of him the weights that he dragged made a wide fluttering on the water, as if he himself were larger. As he swerved, not touching the boat, he saw the more ominous shape of a whaler. It was probably heading for him, having sighted his blowing.

The fishing vessel had started its motor.

The whale headed for the larger vessel with a reckless lunge of mingled anger and pain. He knew that with his weights there would be no escape. Pain from the lances in him made him slow, the fast fishing vessel was going past him, so the whale passed its stern without touching it.

Seconds later, there was an explosion underwater that gave a sensation of pressure on the whale's ears. Great splashes followed, objects fell into the sea, then came the sucking sound of a rush of water. The whale saw a hunk of the fishing vessel, one whole end of it, sinking downward, and he swam away.

Of that eight-man crew there were five survivors, so another story went out: there was a whale in the area with mines attached. Beware! As ever, one survivor said he had seen at least six mines, and the next man said ten. But they agreed that the mines were painted yellow, like some used years ago in the rivers of Korea and Viet Nam. All agreed that the whale had to be destroyed. But no single captain volunteered for the job.

It would take several boats, whalers with harpoon guns, to kill the whale safely. The whalers said they could do it, if ever enough of them got together in the same area as the whale. Three boats might do it, four certainly. But time passed, the whale was not seen where he had been seen, and the idea of a search was abandoned as unprofitable. Every man thought that some other ship would encounter the whale, not his.

The whale was still moving north on a pleasant current. It was the only thing pleasant in his existence now. He was alone and in nagging pain from his many slight wounds, and the mines nagged him also, dragging him from side to side. The chain clinked dully on his head, caught in some stub of a harpoon. All this made him hostile to any life he saw. His dives and his surfacings were slowed by the accursed weights, and on his journey north, he forgot that the weights on him had the power to ward off enemies, until he encountered a certain whaling ship. It had sighted his blow, and at once borne down on him.

Underwater, the whale made a slow arc that would bring him behind the vessel. Then he went on, northward. But the ship was just as near when the whale next came up for air. Without his weights, he thought he could have out-distanced it, been free of it! The ship with its white-frothed prow bore down, and the whale heard the clink of steel and the shouts of men aboard. In anger the whale slashed his tail and aimed for the black hull, but at the last moment he veered nervously left, just brushing the ship with his underbelly, and at once he dived deep.

He heard the dull crack of a harpoon gun.

Louder and deeper came an explosion on his right. The loosely dragging mine on his right had struck the hull of the ship. The timed bomb in the harpoon gun went off harmlessly somewhere to one side and beneath the whale.

The ship had a big rent in it below the water level. It quickly began to sink. Two lifeboats managed to float out, with men aboard, and they picked up other men who were yelling and flailing about in the sea.

The whale swam away from all the confusion, and went on northward. There was now a perceptible difference in weight between his right and left drags: a mine on his right side had disappeared, maybe two had.

The whale left a wake of horror stories, each hanging on the story that had gone before. The ship he had hit was Japanese. There were nine survivors out of a crew of twenty, so fast had the whaler gone down. Their radioman tapped out his message until he was drowned in mid-sentence: STRUCK BY WHALE BEARING MINES. RAPIDLY SINKING LATITUDE ... He had given his position first and had been repeating it with his SOS but, when rescue came, there was nothing to be found save the two lonely lifeboats and their nine. The local seas were alerted against the killer whale. The rescued sailors could not tell how many mines the whale had been carrying, whole chains of them on both sides of him at any rate.

Whalers were asked to destroy the whale at any cost, in their own interests. The whale would be slow because of the mines on him, but he was extremely dangerous, like an armed madman. It made a spectacular news story, even though there were no pictures.

Within twenty-four hours, a hunt was on, and whalers were using searchlights at night to scan the sea's surface. The strategy of the Japanese and Russian vessels was to keep in touch by radio, to go about their usual business but, if the whale was sighted, to announce it to the other ships at once. Then they would encircle the whale and fire harpoon guns and also possibly detonate some of the mines.

The whale was next sighted two hundred nautical miles north of where the Japanese vessel had sunk. The time was 2 in the morning, the dead of night in November in the northern hemisphere, and there was no moon. But the converging ships, some at greater distance than others from their objective, made the seascape almost light, or at least as if flooded with moonlight, milky, grey. The port lights of the little ships weaved and bobbed like drops of blood in the eerie theatre of battle, which covered hundreds of metres at first.

The whale was aware of the lights above him, of the churning noises of the ships' motors which came gradually closer, louder in his ears. He was tired to the point of illogic and desperation. First one ship had pursued him, then a second, and now perhaps there were eight or nine. He was aware that they formed a ring around him. Nothing like this had ever happened before. He breathed while he could, in snatches, preparing himself for a dash to freedom. The circle of light was after all loose and some distance away. Here came the first ship, hard for him.

The whale dived with a flash of his tail in the air. Above and behind him a harpoon gun went off in the water. He swam straight on under and beyond the ring, but the weights hurt him, and finally he had to come up, had to exhale, marking his position, he knew.

And the ships came on quite fast, circling him easily, as if he had covered no distance at all. He would fight. The wind blew hard and cold, and the ships bobbed as they came cautiously toward him. The whale could actually see a harpoon gun swing on one ship, and he dived at once and headed for this vessel. Just at the point of ramming – which the whale would not have done because the ship had a metal hull – the whale swerved left.

Alongside and behind him the weights followed, and one struck the whaler's side below the surface.

A gun-fired harpoon sped through the water above the whale's back, and exploded a few seconds later. The whale rose briefly, seeking a gap through which to escape, but the ships were even closer together. The whale impulsively charged a ship's side, and at the last moment dived under it. There followed another subaqueous boom that wounded a fin of the whale's tail. In fact, the whale began to bleed from this and badly. The sudden pain made the whale veer left, back into the deadly circle. By accident, a mine among those on the whale's left side struck a keel at its exact centre, and tore a hole.

The men on the ships screamed and shouted like mad things. Harpoon guns went off as if fired at random. Two Russian and two Japanese ships were now sinking. The men only half understood one another, but their goal was in common, or had been, to kill the whale. But some commanding officers were now ready to halt the chase in favour of getting out lifeboats and saving their men by transferring them to vessels still afloat.

One man on a Russian ship saw the dread swath of ripples heading directly for his ship and cried out.

The whale was aiming with a painful slowness for the Russian vessel, dived under its hull, and one, maybe two explosions followed as soon as the whale had cleared the other side. This tipped the Russian whaler almost on its beam end, causing a harpoon gun to miss its aim, and the harpoon pierced the breast of a Japanese captain who stood boldly on his tossing deck thirty metres away. The distracted Russian sailor started the winch, and the remains of the Japanese captain were dragged overboard and hauled toward the Russian vessel which was beginning to sink.

'There's *two* whales!' yelled a man in Russian.

'No! *NO!*' came a shrill Japanese voice in Russian. 'Look! There he is again!'

A mine exploded.

As if in retaliation, harpoon guns went off, but they were as likely to hit a man in the water as they were the threshing whale, who had lost his sense of direction, even his picture of the ring now.

The whale charged anywhere. The mines attached to him were still exploding, wherever he struck.

Then a harpoon hit the whale. Internally he burst, and he began to writhe in pain and death, inhaling water.

The winch on the vessel which had fired that harpoon began to turn, dragging the dying whale's body closer. The impact of the mortally wounded whale against the ship's side made hardly a thump, the happy sailor's shouts of triumph rose, then came a terrible *boom*! The handsome brass rail around the gunwale, pride of the Japanese captain, cracked before the eyes of the sailor at the winch, then the deck broke and came up to hit him in the face. Seconds later he slid into the cold sea.

There was nothing of the whale to capture, even to salvage. His tail had been blown off, his vitals scattered by a second harpoon gun. His heavy head had parted from his spinal column, the great head, so full of sperm oil that had been the most valuable part of a whale before the era of petroleum products, sank slowly down, and the human eyes left to see it were not looking.

OPERATION BALSAM; OR
TOUCH-ME-NOT

Three Mile Island had been a catastrophe, a nearly fatal setback, no doubt about that and no use mincing words. It had alerted the American people not only to the fact that nuclear power plants could break down and release radioactive gases into the atmosphere, but also to the fact that government nuclear control authorities gave out lies to the public.

'Nothing to worry about, folks. Everything's under control,' TV and radio had said during the first anxious days, and for weeks afterward too. What American in the country at the time could forget or forgive that? Or the fact that four years later cleanup men could still not enter the chamber where the damaged core was? And that when four men, dressed as if for a moon-walk, did enter the chamber, one collapsed after a few minutes, gripped his head and said he felt awful? Only one sample of nuclear waste, not the desired four, had been snatched from the floor in this costly endeavour.

The fact was that Three Mile Island wasn't cleaned up yet. The fact was the plant owners and regulatory committees were sick of it, and wished it would disappear. But there the towers stood, one of them hopelessly out of commission and even inaccessible.

As if that weren't bad enough for the Nuclear Control Commission, the public had focused its attention on their bureau. The NCC had also lied. No longer could nuclear plants sneak huge trucks by dead of night to garbage dumps in other states, and get back home unnoticed. The trucks might bear a logo of Tidy-Baby Paper Products or Frozen Fish Straight to Your Table, the little old ladies in small towns were looking out of their windows. What were those enormous trucks doing at 3 in the morning creeping through *their* tiny town? The little old ladies and the Boy Scouts wrote letters to their local papers, and things went on from there to the NCC. The NCC had been caught out a few times and reproached by Washington for permitting dumping too close to inhabited areas.

For Benjamin M. Jackson, head of the NCC, existence had become a tightening vice. For the past year, he had had an ulcer which he was only half nursing, because he would not, could not give up his brace of Scotches at the end of the day (if his day had an end) which he felt he had earned and merited. And he could not stop worrying about his job which was damned well-paid and which he didn't want to lose by reminding Washington too often that there simply weren't enough places that he and his staff could okay as dumps for the goddam radioactive crap.

The seas were out of the question, because departing cargoes were too well inspected in case sensitive items got to Russia. Forests had government patrols pretty thick on the ground. One man in the Environmental Watch Agency would have given Benny Jackson the nod for a dumping in Oregon State Park, but he had never been able to guarantee passage through specific patrols at the park, even though Benny had promised to see that the stuff was buried.

Benny was on paper and by oath pledged to guard against careless disposal of nuclear waste, but in fact his job had almost at once turned into one of finding by hook or by crook any place at all where waste could be got rid of. In one of his dreams, Benny had seen himself assigning each man on his Commission – and there were a hundred and thirty-seven – a container of nuclear plant waste to take home every evening and flush down the toilet, but unfortunately radioactive stuff couldn't be handled like that. The public's opinion of nuclear power plants and respect for their efficiency was low and sinking daily. New plants could not easily be built now, because of the intensity of local protests.

Then some genius in Washington, whose name Benny never learned, maybe because it was top-secret, came up with an idea: Washington would donate a football stadium with a track oval and bleachers and a roof to a certain Midwestern university, and under this stadium, below its underground carpark even, radioactive waste would be stored in lead containers, sealed in vast concrete chambers, and be forgotten. 'The area is free from earthquake . . .' read Benny's private memo on the plan. He was to keep this quiet from even his closest colleagues for the nonce. The project was going to be rushed through with no expense spared by the Well-Bilt Construction Company of Minnesota. In a very few months, the memo said, trucks could begin rolling into the sub-basements, because the underground structure would be Well-Bilt's priority.

Benny Jackson's ulcer got a bit better at once. The Well-Bilt people were going to work round the clock and seven days a week.

It was amazing to Benny to read about the stadium-to-be in the newspapers. The university had been quite surprised by the gift from Washington, since the present administration was not known for its generosity to educational institutions. The faculty and students, learning of the size and beauty of their future stadium, sent a huge wreath of flowers to Washington with a ribbon on it saying: 'Mr President, we thank you!' Benny had tears of relief, amusement and nervousness in his eyes when he read that.

Now Benny could afford to say on the telephone, to the requests for dumping sites, that in about two months he would be able to provide space. 'Can you hold it that long?' He knew they would have to hold it longer, that was the way things always went, but it was nice to be able to write or say anything with a ring of truth in it.

Benjamin Jackson was thirty-six, with a small bald spot on his head which otherwise grew straight dark hair. Slender by nature, he was nevertheless developing a paunch. He had a civil engineer's degree from Cornell, and was married with two children. Two years ago, on his appointment as head of the NCC after a reshuffle of its top men, Benny had quit his job in New Jersey with an ecology department and moved with his family to their present home in West Virginia, two miles away from the handsome headquarters of the NCC, which was a two-storey building, formerly a private prep school.

'So the touch-me-not can now be touched,' said Gerald McWhirty when Benny told him about the stadium project. 'Comforting news.'

Gerry McWhirty did not look as pleased as Benny had hoped, but then Gerry wasn't the type to get excited about anything. Gerry hated stalling and lying, and Benny often felt that Gerry didn't like his job. Gerry had a doctorate in physics, but he liked the quiet life, gardening, tinkering with something in his garage, fixing his neighbour's video or anything else that got broken. He was good at plant inspection, though a bit too fussy in Benny's opinion, and Benny had toned down Gerry's reports many a time. Coolant deficiency at a plant in Wilkes-Barre, Benny remembered, and a couple of 'night supervisors' at a plant in Sacramento who Gerry said 'didn't know straight up' about emergency procedures and ought to be replaced. Benny had concurred in regard to the supervisors, but deleted the coolant complaint, because Gerry's figures hadn't seemed to Benny impressive enough for the NCC to mention.

McWhirty often flew with a small staff on inspection tours all over the country. But Benny went alone and incognito to the Midwestern stadium project, because he was curious about its progress.

What Benny saw was gratifying indeed. A vast oval had been dynamited in the earth, earth-moving machines were busy scooping, trucks rolled away laden with soil and rock, and a couple of hundred workmen swarmed at the scene like bees around a hive. And this was a Saturday afternoon.

'Dressing rooms and showers underneath, I suppose,' said Benny to a hard-hat workman, just to get his answer.

'Air-raid shelters too,' replied the workman. 'I should say atomic fallout shelters.' He grinned as if it would never happen.

Benny nodded in a friendly manner. 'Mighty big project. It's gonna be great.'

'You one of the architects?'

'No-o. Just one of the alumni from here.' Benny cast his gaze toward the distant campus on his left as if he loved it. Then, with a good-bye wave to the workman, he went back to his taxi, and returned to the airport.

A month or so later, when Benny thought his ulcer had all but vanished, Love Canal kicked up again. The Environmental Watch Agency reported 'unexpected leakage of chemical waste' from upstream in Love Canal at the city of Niagara Falls, and Benny received a personal letter from some hothead in Washington, DC named Robert V. Clarke, who wrote like a zealot trying to climb the ladder of promotion. Benny would have been willing to bet that Clarke would be bounced off the bottom rung of the ladder very soon, but the letter had been signed also by one of the higher-ups at EWA, because the Love Canal mess contained nuclear wastes as well as 'chemical wastes', a term often used to cover radioactive wastes if a report didn't want to admit outright to radioactivity. The higher-up's signature meant that the NCC had to do something. Some men from the NCC had gone up to examine the Love Canal air and water a year or so ago, had stayed for lunch, Benny recalled, and had okayed what they had seen and analysed: the area was more than safe for human habitation again. Hundreds of families had been evacuated from the area in 1980, when a federal emergency had been declared due to wastes dumped during the 1940s and

1950s. Now Benny's discouraged brain produced, as its first thought: here goes a lot of money if the NCC and the EWA have to launch a new cleanup programme, with more tests to justify a cleanup, and so on. Bloody, effing mess! The only thing good about the letter was the last paragraph which said the 'total review' by the EWA would not be ready before sixteen months from now. But meanwhile the NCC's co-operation and attention was requested. Love Canal, Benny knew, had been taking in thousands of dollars per month as a tourist attraction. Lots of motels, restaurants and foodshops and filling stations were there now and hadn't been there before the hoo-hah. Couldn't the EWA let well enough alone? Benny swallowed a little white pill for his ulcer, just in case. At least the owners of the motels and restaurants weren't going to complain about the latest bad news!

Benny composed and dictated a letter into a machine for his secretary. He said that the unexpected leakage at Love Canal must be due to upstream plants disobeying laws laid down by the NCC and the EWA when his committee headed by Mr So-and-so on such and such a date had visited Love Canal and pronounced the waters free of dangerous pollution. Benny omitted saying that most of the NCC information had come from the owners of a nuclear plant in the area, whose own chemists had made the tests.

Lies, lies, lies! Everyone lied. That was the way Benny justified his lies (which were often merely slantings of facts) to himself. What did trouble him was that he might not lie enough or in the right way to suit Washington, and that some eager beaver, or numbskull, or stooge might raise a stink that would cost Benny his job. Washington always thought it looked good, in case of a scandal or a balls-up somewhere, to replace the head of a regulatory committee. It cooled the public down for a while.

Meanwhile the Three Mile Island cleanup programme officially continued, though in truth nothing had moved since the entry of the four men in space suits several months ago. The man who had collapsed on that occasion had been called, by the owners of the plant, a 'heat stress' victim, and they also said that the millirems he had received were about 75, or 'the equivalent of 2½ chest X-rays'. The other three men had picked up just 190 rems each. The rem (short for millirem) number bearable to the human body was 5,000 per year, a figure set by the federal government. The expensively trained cleanup men in their expensive suits had already received 3,000 each. Now with the radiation level at 200 rems per hour (reduced from 350, said the plant owners), the chief of the cleanup operations had decided that the same cleanup crew could not complete the job without incurring more than the 8,000 set as maximum for workers wearing protective suits.

'That's one of the reasons why the cleanup is so blasted expensive,' one company official had told the journalists. 'All the protection and training and rehearsal that you need to reduce dose rates add very much to the cost of the cleanup which is already past three hundred and eighty million dollars.'

In Benny's opinion, Three Mile Island never would be cleaned up, never, and now it was rather on the back burner, simmering away, no doubt releasing *something* into the surrounding air, but what the hell? It was amazing how many sightseers and curious people drove up as close as they could to the three stacks on Three Mile Island day and night, as if the closer they got, the more excited they felt. It was perhaps like being able to zoom up to a car accident when the victim still lay on the street, or to a fire still burning in a big building. One newspaper said that GPU, the owners of the plant, were 'promoting' Three Mile Island as a tourist mecca.

Thanks to Gerald McWhirty, the university stadium project received a code name, Operation Balsam. The touch-me-not plant, so called because of its explosive fruit, was also the garden balsam, Gerry explained. Operation Balsam sounded innocuous, and Benny liked it.

At the end of June a director of Well-Bilt sent Benny a letter saying that all was going very well and ahead of schedule, and that part of the basement was already in use.

'I don't know how all that concrete can be dry so soon,' Gerry McWhirty said to Benny when they met by accident at the coffee dispenser in the corridor.

Benny glanced around him. Not every person in the building knew about Operation Balsam or was meant to. 'Well-Bilt must be doing things right. They're getting all the money they need.'

'That's something, at least. That was what was the matter with Three Mile Island, you know, builders doing everything on the cheap. Those container rooms for Balsam have to be airtight, with not a millimetre allowable for subsidence.'

Benny knew. McWhirty's remarks might have worried Benny a

little, but he refused to be worried. Operation Balsam was the only cheerful thing in his life now.

There was plenty uncheerful, and annoying. The same day that McWhirty had made his remark, Benny's hotline telephone rang from Washington.

'Hello, Benny. Matt here. You know the cleanup crew at Three Mile Island?'

'The four men who went in, you mean?' Benny imagined the sick one worse and in some hospital, launching a lawsuit against the plant owners.

'Yeah, well, there's a lot more of them on the operation, fellows in the control room, women too. They all decided to go to California together on a junket. Whooping it up, you know? I warn you now, because you'll maybe get some flak at your office about it. It'll be on TV news tonight and I didn't want it to shock you.'

'Junket – why?' Benny asked.

'Who knows? They're all on a high, we heard. Either drunk or sniffing coke. Got to sign off now, Benny.'

Benny did watch the 6 o'clock news. The anchorman of the programme tried to put a happy face on it. '. . . tired workers on the Three Mile Island cleanup operations got together to take a well-earned break today, flying first-class from Philadelphia to San Francisco, and they look as happy as – ha-ha! – Legionnaires on a junket to Atlantic City in the old days! What is your name, please, sir?'

A swimmy-faced man uttered an unintelligible name that sounded like Joe Olsen, but it could have been George O'Brien. 'Live it down, live it up!' Olsen or O'Brien said, interrupting the anchorman merrily. '*Tha's* our motto! Yip-pee-ee!'

'We're gonna contaminate ourselves a li'l more!' a woman with smeared lipstick contributed.

'Just good clean fun!' said the laughing anchorman to his TV audience.

'My God! The goddam media trying to get at us *again*! Washington ought to put 'em out of business!' Benny scowled at his shocked wife for an instant before heading for the Scotch bottle in the kitchen.

The rest of what the thirty or so men and women had to say about their junket was not printed in the *New York Times* or the *Washington Post*, who did mention their holiday, but it was in the *Village Voice* and

Rolling Stone, and that was that they considered themselves 'hopelessly contaminated by radioactivity'. They had been carrying home rems in their clothing, their hair, on their skin for weeks, all for higher pay and danger money; they felt that their homes and families had been contaminated too, that they themselves might live a few more years, but who knew for how long or what might happen? So, before their hair started falling out and nausea kept them from enjoying their food, they were going to live it up. Their motto was repeated.

My God, why wouldn't it all just go away, Benny thought. His ulcer was back in full force. He couldn't tell his wife about the one bright spot, Operation Balsam, but he had to tell her about his ulcer, because he could not eat some of the dishes that she prepared.

Presumably the junketeers straggled back home after a time in quieter fashion than they had departed. But the word spread. Some of them were interviewed again, and rated a column in *Time* and *Newsweek*. They stuck to their story. The owners of the Three Mile Island plant had sacked the lot of them, but the mutinous thirty-odd to a man and woman said they were glad to have been fired. They denounced the 'filthy coverup' by the owners and the NCC and even the EPA, which ought to be concerned now with the radioactivity leaking out and damaging trees, livestock and any people dumb enough to be within twenty miles of the place.

Benny Jackson's office laboriously composed another form letter, using all the favourable facts they could find, and Benny was not even sure they were facts, but at least they had been printed in the *Post* of September 1983 in the same item that had reported less favourable information which Benny was not using. He quoted:

The spokesman for the owners of the Three Mile Island plant report that their 'dose reduction program', designed to reduce radiation doses to cleanup workers, had cut radiation dose rates on the ground floor of the container building from 350 millirems per hour to about 200 at present.

Benny did wonder, as he dictated the statement, how the owners or anybody could reduce radiation except by letting it escape, say by just opening a window a little.

Gerald McWhirty looked over the letter at Benny's request, rubbed his reddish moustache, and nodded without comment.

'I think it's not bad,' Benny said.

'A mess,' McWhirty said. 'That's my comment on Three Mile Island. Built on the cheap, everyone knows that.'

A vague patriotism stirred shame in Benny. America doing something on the cheap! England, France and Germany seldom if ever had trouble with their nuclear power plants, certainly no catastrophic troubles, because they did things the expensive and correct way. Benny was glad that McWhirty didn't say this now, because McWhirty had in the past.

Operation Balsam was completed in late July. The NCC received an invitation from Well-Bilt. 'Our installations are now in place. We welcome you at any time to a private and informal preview and inspection.'

Benny at first did not want to go, because his name and face were known to the media, and suppose some of them were there? Even on the ground's surface? 'This isn't an official opening of the football field too, is it?' he asked McWhirty, who had been on the telephone with Well-Bilt.

'Certainly not. I wouldn't be caught dead there at the stadium opening. It's just Operation Balsam.'

At the last moment, Benny did go, because Douglas Ferguson, an NCC director and a good friend of McWhirty's, said, 'Grab an old raincoat and come with us, Benny. Just about fifteen of us. Take-off at ten tomorrow morning, and we'll be home before midnight.'

So Benny did grab an old raincoat, because it was a bit of a disguise. He looked not the least important in it.

The NCC men were met at the Indianapolis airport by four limousines laid on by Well-Bilt.

Little pennants flew around the rim of the stadium roof, which resembled a huge half-eggshell. In the brilliant sunshine, the surrounding turf shone like emerald.

'Beautiful!' Benny exclaimed, bowled over by the changes since he had seen the place such a short time ago.

A huge truck painted plain white had turned off the road just behind them, and Benny watched it approach a clump of trees on the lawn, tilt downward, and roll out of sight. That was one of *them*, Benny knew, loaded with radioactive junk. His heart leapt with a rare sense of success. Since the sub-basement was purported to be a fallout shelter, hospital and so on, the trucks could presumably be carrying dried foodstuffs, blankets, and medical supplies.

'Service entrance,' McWhirty murmured with a smile at Benny, having seen the direction of Benny's glance.

Uniformed and armed guards met them at a gate and waved their cars through. A neatly dressed middle-aged man introduced himself as Frank Marlucci, a supervisor for Well-Bilt. They all walked into one of the broad entrances for spectators. There were ticket booths, benches, elevators.

'I suppose you'd like to see the basements first?' asked Mr Marlucci.

They would. The elevator went down and down, past CHANGING ROOMS and CARPARK, and they all got out into a concrete corridor whose ceiling was some fifteen feet high. Off this corridor led broader passages, wide enough for trucks. Arrows on the walls indicated vehicle movement direction.

'This way, please, gentlemen,' said Mr Marlucci.

Benny could hear a truck grinding in low gear somewhere. In a central room from which passageways radiated, they now saw the big lead containers being fork-lifted from the back of a white truck. Another fork-lift was depositing containers gently on to a conveyor belt. The containers disappeared in the distance like suitcases at an airport after a passenger had checked in. Benny's face spread in a smile. It all looked so wonderfully solid, so buried, so impregnable!

Even Gerry McWhirty seemed impressed. 'And the rooms? The storerooms?' he asked Mr Marlucci, shouting over the din.

Mr Marlucci beckoned, and they all began to walk. 'This one, for example.' He stopped at a steel door some ten feet square, unlocked a metal cover to the right of it, and worked a combination lock by pressing numbers. The door slid to the right into the concrete wall. 'This room's nearly full. Not quite.'

Benny couldn't judge the room's size, because the big rectangular containers lined the walls in triple or quadruple layers, and reached to the ceiling at the back. He saw McWhirty hesitate a moment, then step into the room.

McWhirty looked around at the containers, at the concrete floor and stamped on it, as if his flyweight compared to the containers' could make a difference or a shudder in the construction. 'May I see it closed again?' McWhirty asked as he walked out.

Mr Marlucci pressed a button and the door slid shut.

McWhirty ran his finger or his fingernail along the side of the door at the bottom. 'A little space here.'

Mr Marlucci shook his head emphatically. 'The door's grooved, sir, touching at the bottom – countersunk, airtight in steel housing.'

Benny wanted to ask how long the lead containers were supposed to last, but he was supposed to know. Benny knew the containers were more than a foot thick – fantastic – and that seemed made for eternity.

Farther along in the corridor, McWhirty noticed a crack in a concrete wall, and ran his finger along it.

'That's going to be fixed,' said Mr Marlucci. 'That's normal for now.'

The rooms were twenty metres square, Mr Marlucci replied to a question from one of the NCC men. He led them to the Facilities Room, another square concrete-walled room with a blue floor, a counter with stools, cooking facilities, refrigerators, tables and chairs, restrooms, a cigarette vending machine – a scene now eerily barren of a human figure.

'They're going to stick a few posters up,' said Mr Marlucci with a smile, 'so it won't look so bleak. It's really just the Balsam workers' canteen, so it doesn't have to look like a happy-hour bar.'

McWhirty wanted to see another container room. 'Maybe on the other side of the basement?'

The group began a walk equal to the breadth of the football field above them, Benny supposed, and possibly more. They had to flatten themselves against a wall to let a fork-lift roll by with six containers on it. Benny imagined that he felt the floor shake under him. Was there another basement below this? Small red tanks were fixed at intervals along these walls, and Benny thought they were fire extinguishers until on closer inspection he saw that they were labelled oxygen. A headgear like an old-fashioned gas mask topped each red tank, and the apparatus was sealed in a transparent plastic bubble. At another steel door in a row of doors, Mr Marlucci stopped, and again worked a digital lock.

'How full is the basement now?' McWhirty asked. 'A quarter? A third?'

'More than half, sir,' Mr Marlucci replied as the steel door rolled into the wall. 'Amazing how fast it's filling up. But then the trucks're coming in day and night since – oh, nearly a month.'

Now Benny's spirits sank a little. At this rate, they wouldn't be able to use Balsam for two or three urgent jobs that were on Benny's mind. 'Where's it all coming from – mainly?' Benny asked, feeling suddenly like a landlord whose apartment had been taken over by a family larger than had been agreed upon.

'Oh, you'd be surprised, sir. We have orders – top-secret, of course – from Washington to admit this and that from Texas, California, Ohio, anywhere at all they're having trouble. They're not labelled when they get here, but if they're in the right containers, we're obliged to take 'em in.'

Benny fumed in silence. Washington had higher authority, of course, but why hadn't Washington or the EWA told the NCC that they were cramming the place?

McWhirty had entered the half-full room whose door had opened, and was looking around at the walls he could see, at the corners of the lead containers. 'You've got a flashlight, haven't you, Doug? Check the back wall for cracks and moisture as far as you can.'

Douglas Ferguson pulled a flashlight from his pocket and walked in.

'At this rate,' McWhirty said to Mr Marlucci, 'this basement will be full in another month?'

'This sub-basement,' said Mr Marlucci, smiling. 'Well – I'd say another three to four weeks. We'll have it full and sealed before the football season.'

Awful, Benny thought. Washington would simply have to donate a stadium to another university somewhere, and as soon as possible.

They were drifting on toward the exit on the side of the basement they had not seen, where Mr Marlucci said they could take an elevator up to the ground level and see the stadium interior.

On the earth's surface, on the sunlit grass, Mr Marlucci shook his head as he spoke to a man in shirtsleeves and blue jeans who had asked him something. Benny was close enough to hear Mr Marlucci say:

'The fallout shelters're pretty empty now, nothing much to see yet. We're bringing in supplies, as you see.'

To Benny Mr Marlucci said, as they walked up a ramp, 'One of the professors from the university. Now here we have a view!' With widespread arms Mr Marlucci beheld the football field as if he would embrace it.

A dark grey running track framed the green of the football field. Bleachers climbed up and up, empty yet poised and focused for drama.

'Really something!' said a voice among the NCC men.

Mr Marlucci talked about the heating and ventilation systems, the First Aid room for players and for spectators if they needed it, and finally he suggested drinks and a snack at a nearby restaurant, if the gentlemen had time. The NCC men hadn't. It was after 4 now, and their plane left at 6:15. The afternoon had flown.

The limousines arrived again, congratulations, thanks and goodbyes were exchanged, and the cars moved off for the airport.

Benny Jackson sat next to McWhirty on the aeroplane, because he wanted to hear McWhirty's impressions while they were still fresh.

'We'll look at it again in two weeks,' said McWhirty. 'Take a rem check ourselves downstairs and at all the vents. Those cracks –' McWhirty gave a laugh. 'Talk about a rush job! I want to speak with Doug.' He unfastened his seat belt and got up.

Benny heard McWhirty's voice behind him in the aisle asking, 'Where's Doug?'

'Doug?' said another voice. 'Maybe he went to the lav.'

A couple of minutes later McWhirty bent over Benny with a pained expression on his face. 'Doug's not on the plane. It just occurs to me –'

'What?' asked Benny.

McWhirty sat down stiffly. 'I didn't see him since he went into that container room. Do you suppose he got locked in there?'

'Christ, no!' Benny said at once, and thought back. 'I didn't see Marlucci close that door.'

'Neither did I, but – I just checked with the fellows and nobody remembers seeing him at the airport just now. He's back there, Benny!' With difficulty Gerry kept his voice low.

'We'll phone Well-Bilt as soon as we land.'

'We could radio now. It's a couple of hours till we land.'

'No,' said Benny, meaning the idea of radioing from the plane and asking for a container room to be opened. 'No.'

They both ordered Scotches.

'Doug'll probably phone tonight from some hotel in Indianapolis,' Benny said. 'Maybe he went to a toilet in that sub-basement and got lost from us.'

It was close to 10 p.m. before they got to a telephone at the West Virginia airport. Benny was told that Frank Marlucci had left at 5:30.

'I'd like to speak to someone in charge of the sub-basement. This is Benjamin Jackson of NCC. It's urgent.'

After some delay, and much offering of more coins by the NCC men who stood outside the booth, another male voice came on, and Benny again identified himself. 'I and some colleagues were visiting the sub-basement today. I have reason to think one of our party may be locked in one of the container rooms. I'd like someone to take a look *now*.'

A pause. 'We get a lot of joke calls from the students, sir. We'll need some more identification before we – We're very busy here, sir. Good night.' The man hung up.

One of the NCC men said that maybe Doug had got out, if he had ever been in, and would phone Gerry or Benny tonight, and come back on the morning plane tomorrow. Benny and Gerry agreed that they should go home, wait for a call, but also try the two Well-Bilt-Balsam numbers again tonight.

From his own house, McWhirty telephoned Evelyn Ferguson, Doug's wife, and told her that Doug had had to stay overnight in Indianapolis to talk some details over with construction people.

Benny and Gerry McWhirty were stonewalled by the male voices that answered the telephones in the small hours of the night at the stadium. They didn't know anything about a party of visitors having inspected the stadium and 'the basements' in the afternoon, and 'Operation Balsam' produced no glimmer of recognition. The NCC, if such they were, should get in touch with the Frank Marlucci they were asking about tomorrow, and he could verify matters and take care of their requests.

'What on earth is the matter?' asked Benny's wife Beatrice, coming into the living-room at 2 in the morning.

'Doug Ferguson – as I said – he hasn't got all the info he needs for tomorrow and I can't find what hotel he's at.'

When Benny telephoned Well-Bilt at 9:30 the same morning, he learned that Mr Marlucci was not coming to work that day. 'Mr Siegman then, please.' Benny had a short list of names of the Well-Bilt people.

'Mr Siegman's in conference now, sir. Everyone's in conference, because the press is due this afternoon to look at the stadium.'

'Who's in charge of the container rooms – *now?*' Benny asked.

Silence. 'We've only got a skeleton staff here, sir. No one person's in charge.'

'Someone like Marlucci. Look, this is urgent. I have reason to think one of our party may be locked in one of the container rooms – since yesterday and he's got to be let out!'

'Wh-which room, sir?'

'Can't tell you exactly. On the other side from where the trucks roll down. On the left side as you go along what I think is the main corridor to the other side.' Benny had the plans before him, but the passages and rooms had no numbers or letters on them. The passages radiated from the centre but were crossed by circles of passages that intersected them, making the plan look rather like a spider's web, but he thought the corridor they had been in was central, so he called it the main corridor.

'There's a delivery entrance for trucks both sides, sir.'

'It's not too much trouble for you to open those rooms and have a look, is it? It's one of the half-full rooms. Do that and call me back, would you?' Benny made sure the man had his number correct.

The man did not ring back.

Doug Ferguson did not arrive on the morning plane from Indianapolis. Benny had begun chewing his minty pills, the only pain-reliever he had until he renewed his prescriptions. Gerald McWhirty was at work with a team on the NCC's 'Preliminary Report on Operation Balsam'. This was for EWA and it had to be favourable and at least sixty pages long. Marlucci had given them a sheaf of papers, which could be organised and copied. Evelyn Ferguson rang the office twice to ask if Doug were back or had communicated.

'It's not like him not to phone,' Evelyn said. 'He can phone me at any hour day or night, and he always does.'

'I know it's a heavy assignment he's got out there,' Benny said. 'He probably hasn't a minute free.'

From 2 p.m. onward that afternoon, the two Well-Bilt numbers simply didn't answer. Benny imagined the sub-basement, where the phones perhaps were, sealed off from the journalists, with no trucks rolling today, not a soul down there except Doug maybe, shouting unheard in a container room. Had the last man he had spoken to believed him about a man maybe locked in a container room?

Benny Jackson and Gerry McWhirty lingered in the NCC building after everyone else had gone home. McWhirty looked haggard, and admitted that he hadn't slept the night before. They decided to try again to reach Marlucci. Benny got busy with information on one telephone and McWhirty on another, trying to get the home number of Marlucci, who must live in the area, though it was conceivable that he had rented an apartment for the duration of the Well-Bilt job, and wouldn't be listed yet. He'd still have a telephone, Benny reasoned. Neither Indianapolis nor any town in the area had a number for Frank Marlucci. Was that really his name, Benny wondered?

It was Benny's turn to have a sleepless night. Benny had said to McWhirty that he would go to the stadium on the plane tomorrow Thursday, and McWhirty had said no, he would go, because he was less conspicuous than the head of NCC. Benny now saw Doug's incarceration as a stupid accident, indicating inefficiency. That was how Washington would see it. It reflected upon Benny and the Nuclear Control Commission.

Nevertheless, Benny picked up his telephone the first thing Thursday morning, and rang his Washington hotline, thinking himself rather noble for putting his job at risk by doing so.

'Jackson, NCC. Is Matt there?' Matt Schwartz was a man Benny often talked to, a friendly and helpful fellow, though Benny had never met him face to face. Now he was told that Matt was in conference in another building and could not be reached. 'This is about Operation Balsam . . . Yes . . . Specifically we have to find a certain Frank Marlucci, one of the superintendents for Well-Bilt. We have to speak with him on the phone and we can't locate him.' Benny's tone sounded firm, but he had faltered: he had not said straightaway that an NCC man appeared to have been locked up in a container room since Tuesday afternoon.

'What do you want him for?' asked Washington.

'I need to ask him something. He wasn't at work – yesterday.' Benny had not tried this morning, he realised.

'Call you back,' said Washington, and hung up.

Washington was back in record time, the same male voice. 'Marlucci is no longer employed by Well-Bilt, sir. No use trying to reach him.'

'They must have his home number. I need to ask him – '

'We know about that. The trouble.'

Benny was surprised. 'And something's been done about it?'

'Yes, sir,' said the voice crisply.

'This has to do with Douglas Ferguson of NCC. You mean he's all right?'

'All right? What's the matter with him?'

'Wh-what did you mean by "the trouble" out there?'

'Marlucci did something wrong and got fired. We don't advise any of our people to go out there for a while. Till further notice.'

Those were orders, Benny knew. He had just time to catch Gerry McWhirty at home and tell him not to take the morning plane. McWhirty came into the office at 11. The Well-Bilt numbers were now answering, but Benny had not been able to speak with anyone who could tell him Marlucci's personal number, or who knew if any container rooms had been opened yesterday or today to look for a man who might have been locked in one. People simply didn't know anything.

'This is Jackson of NCC,' Benny repeated to one man.

'We *understand*, sir. We can't help you.'

Once more Benny and Gerry had a faint hope that Doug might come in on the plane that arrived at 11:30. If so, he didn't telephone, and they hadn't the courage to phone his wife and ask if Doug had got home. Evelyn had rung once that morning to ask if NCC had any news, and Benny told his secretary to tell Mrs Ferguson that they hadn't heard from Doug either, but were assuming he would be back Saturday latest. Benny knew this was not going down well with Evelyn Ferguson.

The afternoon brought a further torment. Inhabitants of the Love Canal area had organised a new campaign, and starting after lunch the NCC offices were bombarded with telephone calls and telegrams from homeowners and housewives angry at having been told they had to move out again, after having been told they could move back to their once abandoned homes and apartments. The Committee for Justice at Love Canal tied up the telephones with personal calls and telegrams being read by telegraph office operators – all the messages blaming the NCC for misinformation and lies – until Benny thought he was going mad. A bomb should hit the goddam Love Canal area and their whole effing committee too!

On Friday Benny was informed by a female voice on his hotline from Washington that Frank Marlucci had been killed in a car accident yesterday afternoon in southern Indiana. Benny knew what had most likely happened: someone had deliberately run Marlucci off the road. Benny felt sickish, then reminded himself that he had heard about such things before, two or three times before. He knew why he was feeling sickish: Marlucci's death confirmed Doug's death. Benny was sick at the thought of Doug in that room half-full of containers, Doug getting weaker from thirst and hunger, from lack of air, moaning unheard, dying. Benny called McWhirty in to tell him.

'Good Christ.' McWhirty sank into a leather chair in Benny's office as if all his strength had gone.

'You think maybe Marlucci tried to get him out?' Benny asked. 'Or did get him out – dead?'

'Or loaders found him and Marlucci got the blame.' McWhirty looked drugged, but was merely exhausted. 'I figure Doug would've been dead by yesterday morning from asphyxiation.'

There was no use in trying to figure out exactly what had happened, Benny supposed. 'You think they'll just hush it up – if they found him?'

'Yes,' Gerry said.

The Well-Bilt people with their machinery would know how to get rid of a body, Benny was sure. 'What'll we tell his wife?'

McWhirty looked miserable. 'We'll have to tell her he dis-appeared – that he's maybe dead. I'll tell her. You know – our job has its hazards.'

'We'll make sure she gets a generous pension,' said Benny.

McWhirty went into a daze or depression which he could not shake off, but he still came to the office. He would not take a week's leave, even though his doctor ordered it.

In the following week a torrent of letters and a two-day picketing of the NCC grounds – which did much damage to the pretty lawns, what with the police trying to wrestle the more unruly protesters off the premises – disturbed the whole staff of NCC, and caused them to come to work in armoured cars which they crawled into at 8:30 in the morning at appointed places. The demonstrators called them-selves the New CIO or Citizens in Outrage, and the nucleus of them seemed to have come from the Three Mile Island district, but they were aiming to make Outrage a nationwide movement by teaming up with militant environmentalists. The NCC came to work and departed in a shower of stones, eggs, epithets and threats.

One day in late September, Gerald McWhirty drove his car, the older of the two he and his wife owned, over the edge of a highway into a valley and killed himself. He left no note behind. It was called an accident.

Evelyn Ferguson, who had been drinking quite a bit since her husband's disappearance (as it was called), was admitted to a rehabilitation centre in Massachusetts at government expense. Benny wrote her cheerful postcards, when he remembered to do so.

The NCC came up with an affirmative report on Operation Balsam for Washington, when the site got its official inspection in October. Benny was there, and saw even worse cracks in the concrete than McWhirty had, but Well-Bilt promised to repair them, so the cracks were not mentioned in the report. Still worse, a rem count taken by the NCC at various vents on the exterior of the stadium detected 210 per hour at one, 300-odd at another, and so on, with only one of the twelve vents clean. Where was the radioactive stuff coming from? Well-Bilt promised to look into it, but meanwhile said it believed that the rem discharge was not high enough to cause alarm or to do perceptible damage to human, animal or plant life in the vicinity.

Benny had other problems now. A plutonium shipment, code-named the Italian Shipment because it had nothing to do with Italy, out of Houston bound for South Carolina, had disappeared, and could the NCC look into this and see if a friendly country had stolen it, or what? This made at least four lost shipments on land and sea that Benny's office was supposed to find. Benny missed Gerry McWhirty in a strange way, as if Gerry had been the voice of his conscience, which was now silenced. He missed Doug Ferguson too, but in a different way. He remembered the interesting rust-red tweed jacket that Doug had worn that last day, remembered complimenting Doug on it. Now Doug was sealed up, probably, and if so, for ever. All the container rooms had been filled and the term used by Well-Bilt was 'permanently and hermetically sealed'. Benny's ulcer was no better, but no worse either, and he had managed the inspection day at Operation Balsam quite well: he had vowed to himself not to wince, not even to think about Doug Ferguson's corpse maybe lying behind one of those square steel doors that he walked past that day, and he had succeeded.

NABUTI: WARM WELCOME
TO A UN COMMITTEE

Nature and Lady Luck had smiled upon the broad and fertile land of Nabuti, in West Africa. Nabuti had rivers, lush plains, a seacoast of more than a thousand miles, and in the hills there was copper. For two hundred years Nabuti had been exploited by the white man, who had mined, and built roads and ports and railways to service them. Before the first half of the twentieth century was over, Nabuti had five thousand miles of paved roads, rivers had been dredged and banked for ships and boats, electricity and water systems installed, schools started. Malaria and bilharziasis had been conquered, general health much improved, and most of the many infants lived.

Nabuti won its independence in the 1950s by merely asking for it. Independence was in the air all over Africa, like a champagne that could be inhaled. A cadre of whites stayed on for a while in Nabuti to make sure everything was functioning properly, that crews knew how to run the railroads, repair electric power plants, service machinery from tractors to bicycles, but the whites were not popular during this period. The sooner they left, the better was the idea, and the whites got the idea after being spat on in the streets a few times by idle youths, then – several of them – attacked and beaten to death. The whites left.

There was a half-year-long party or festival then, while four or five contestants for leadership made speeches to the public, saying how they would run the country. Each of them promised a lot. They had to orate over the noise of jukeboxes and transistor radios. There was a voting of sorts, then a run-off between the two leading contestants, an argument about the vote-counting, and a husky young man in his twenties named Bomo came out the victor, because he was chief of police and the police were armed. The police, originally trained by the whites, would make a good cadre for the formation of a Nabutian army, the white administrators had said,

53

and that is what happened. The police force became an ever-growing army, and with the millions of dollars bequeathed to Nabuti to launch it as an independent African state, and the yearly gifts and loans since, the purchase of snappy uniforms, rifles, machineguns and tanks was no problem at all. Bomo, who had never been awakened by a 6 a.m. bugle in his life, appointed himself General-in-Chief of the army, besides being President. Armed force, armed menacing was necessary, because Bomo intended to make his people work. Progress – the word to Bomo meant more comfort, higher medical standards, more exports of copper, more cars and TV sets – progress had to continue.

A few white construction workers arrived by invitation to get some projects started: Bomo's Government House for one, and his private dwelling, the Small Palace, for another, a few high-rise apartment buildings to house workers in the capital Goka, and also a bigger airport terminus and longer runways, because Bomo had tourism in mind. Wages for manual labour were at first good, attracting people from the farms to the cities. Then the inevitable happened: basic foods ran short, and Nabuti had to start importing food, not a terrible burden because rice, wheat and dried milk were fairly given away by an arrangement with a United Nations agency. Worst was the copper mines' condition. The miners had grown ever more undisciplined, absenteeism could not be controlled, there was drunkenness on beer mainly, and a constant demand for higher wages resulting in half-strikes or disorganised strikes which within two or three years had slowed production down to twenty percent of normal. If a piece of machinery broke down, an angry worker would profess not to know how to repair it, and maybe he didn't.

Nabuti appealed for more financial aid and got it. Bomo realised full well that his people wanted refrigerators, TV sets, private cars and flush toilets in just about that order. He got the TV sets, millions of them, at remarkably low cost, a tiny sum to be added to the national debt. The TV kept the population quieter as to labour unrest, though more and more people simply did not come to work, but stayed home watching TV. Those whose sets had broken down went to the houses of friends whose sets hadn't broken down. Life had turned into one big TV and beer party in the capital because, thanks to satellite pick-up, the TV sets were showing something twenty-four hours a day, and the Nabutians didn't much care what language it was in, as long as there was a picture on the screen.

Other problems existed: traffic jams, for instance. People paid no attention to red and green lights, first with the excuse that nobody else paid attention, then on the fact (it was a fact) that most of the lights were not working anyway. The main avenues of Goka bore stagnant streams of private cars, trucks, and an occasional farm tractor, a popular means of transport, because a tractor could push anything else out of its path, and could glide over potholes and manholes without covers. Lots of cars broke down due to overheating in these traffic snarls, and cars were often abandoned and became cannibalised hulks a couple of hours later. There was no service for removal of these ruined cars, so they stayed a long while. A shantytown of unemployed and houseless people had built up a ring around Goka and around two or three other large towns too. Smoke from garbage burning and a stench from open gutter sewage wafted at all times over Goka no matter which way the wind was blowing. When no wind blew, a smog hung, almost obscuring the national flag atop Government House, which was six storeys high. The telephone system worked just enough for some people to keep trying to use it, though usually their dialling, despite a dial tone sometimes, got them nowhere. Consequently footrunners were in demand. Young boys and a few young girls would deliver letters or more often verbal messages, packages, and groceries and black market goods to people who lived in the high-rises and stayed there for safety reasons and because the elevators did not work. A handful of people had plenty of money, but the majority were hungry. The people with money were in or connected with the army, the black market, prostitution or drugs.

Business and commerce had almost ceased to exist, and Bomo had given up, though he had never told himself this consciously and directly. His job, he told himself, was to hold his country together, to be in touch with regional groups, the strong men (on his side) who could quell disorder, and stamp out the roving bands of adolescents who robbed people and looted stores, to make a twice-yearly report to the United Nations on health progress, and blame lack of agricultural and industrial progress on drought, strikes, and disruptions caused by adjacent countries' belching their own hungry and unemployed into Nabuti, right over the borders, despite machinegun fire from Nabuti's soldiers against them. These intruders took to the bush, then insinuated themselves among the squatters that ringed the big cities. It was disgusting. But the United

Nations people seemed to believe Bomo when he said he was doing his best. At any rate, the money kept coming.

Bomo, six foot four in his youth, had grown heavier with the years. Now at nearly fifty-two he had a two-metre girth, and ordered extra long Sam Browne belts so that four or more empty holes remained for the tongue of his belt buckle to slide into, in case he ever needed them. Such attention to detail made a man look good, he thought. He had two dozen medals which he wore when making speeches, several caps with abundant gold braid, and a high-necked, gold-braided tunic uniform for the most important occasions such as military reviews. He seldom wore full uniforms, because they were uncomfortable in the heat. But he always wore khaki trousers, not shorts, and on most days an open-necked army shirt with sleeves rolled up, and sandals without socks. In this gear he was driven every morning in a jeep on a zigzagging tour of inspection of Goka and its surrounds. This took from about 10 a.m. until 1 p.m., when it was time to go back to his Small Palace for lunch and an afternoon rest. Three soldiers with rifles in hand rode standing in the jeep, on the lookout for trouble and also to give a show of armed power, though it had been years since they had had to fire a shot. The populace now stood on street corners talking, and sat on kerbs drinking coffee or beer. Bomo's morning round had another purpose, to drop in for half an hour on two or three mistresses, or wives as he had to call them when speaking to foreign diplomats. Bomo couldn't count his sons, maybe seventy-five, maybe a hundred. The number of his daughters didn't matter, though the country was full of girls who claimed that he was their father, so many that the claim was now worthless.

Bomo's favourite sons were two, by different mothers, one named Kuo, about eighteen, the other Paulo, the same age give or take a couple of months. Both were keen to be their father's successor, and they lived in the Small Palace with their wives, who numbered three or four each. Bomo played them off against each other, urging them to vie for severity against insurrection, and to shoot first, which was what it took to rule Nabuti. One of them would kill the other one day, then Bomo would know that his country would fall into the right hands, those of the stronger man.

One day a runner brought Bomo a sealed envelope, much smudged, with the United Nations' insignium on its back. The letter was a month old, Bomo's old translator informed him, and the substance of it was that fifteen members of the UN African Aid Committee and five aides would like to pay a visit to Nabuti on such and such a date which was now only nine days off. The letter said that the Committee had been unable to reach Government House or the Small Palace by telephone, and that this letter was the second dispatched, and the writer hoped that it would reach its destination, and requested confirmation, if possible, at Hotel Green Heaven in Gibbu, which was the capital of Gibbi, a country adjacent to Nabuti on its eastern border, and with which Nabuti had such bad relations that Bomo doubted that any message from his country would be delivered.

There was no way of avoiding this visit, Bomo realised. The Committee was visiting several countries in the area on this same tour, their first in five years. To create a civil war – easily done – would make his government look worse, even though it might prevent the visit for security reasons.

Bomo summoned his two sons.

'Clean everything up!' Bomo said in his native language, and used a few French and English words as he went on. 'Garbage, beer cans, *merde*, *bidonvilles*, beggars and thieves! Shoot them and burn the corpses! After that, the streets must be cleaned, the windows washed! And the airport! Clear those runways!'

Kuo and Paulo spoke to their strongmen in the army, and these sent out squads to enforce faster garbage burning, street clearing and sweeping, the rinsing of sewers and the digging of gutters for that, the shooting of recalcitrant citizenry and those too leprous or otherwise too awful-looking to be beheld. All hands in the nation turned to this formidable task which had to be done in nine days. Laggards would be shot by firing squad. Within hours, the air of Goka and of the other three large towns of the country was full of rifle fire, shouts, smoke, and the rasp of metal as car bodies were dragged by manpower from the streets.

Bomo gave his personal attention to the Hotel Bomo and to Government House, whither he had decided the Committee should be taken in that order after arrival at Bomo Airport. There would be a banquet in the largest salon of Government House's ground floor, so the big kitchens in the back of the building had to be readied for this. Government House had been constructed in the style of the Parthenon as to its façade, because of a remark in a speech a white man had made on departing from Nabuti, that there would be a 'future house of government noble as the Parthenon'. Bomo had charged a French architect with this, and the architect had been exasperated, Bomo remembered, because Bomo had wanted a six-storey edifice, including the two-storey-high pillars and the even higher pediment in which Bomo wanted a balcony also. The balcony in the pediment existed, and from it Bomo had made many speeches in the past, but now Government House was out of use except as an unofficial recreation centre. This had begun with the sentries playing cards, finally snooker, then had come jukeboxes and drink dispensers, more and more cots for sleeping, and a well-patronised brothel. A couple of rooms on the first floor still held the papers and files with which the country had begun its independence but, as no one paid taxes even under pressure and receipts were impossible to get for incoming machinery and shipments of any-thing, employees had long ago drifted off and disappeared, after drinking the vast cellars out of whisky and wine. Most windows in Government House were broken, the electrical system was 'out' or 'down', and the elevators did not work even when the electricity was on. Bomo called for his best electricians.

'I want these lights on and the air-conditioning on in twenty-four hours!' he yelled at the six frightened men on the steps of Government House.

Women were already sweeping and mopping and washing the walls inside, while soldiers prodded out idlers and squealing prostitutes at bayonet point.

Lulu-Fey, one of Bomo's wives and current favourite, was practising her belly dance, which she had learned on a trip to Tunisia with Bomo. It was not a native dance of Nabuti, but Bomo had told her that Western men enjoyed watching it, and that she should dance as a surprise for their honoured guests after the banquet, and Lulu-Fey was happy to oblige. She had already been helpful in planning the menu which was to centre around roast pig and piglet.

The telephone technicians after two days managed to reconnect the line between Government House and the Small Palace, and the first call Bomo got was from the UN Committee, saying that they had been trying to get through for weeks, and was their proposed date agreeable? Bomo assured them that it was.

Tom-toms beat day and night to inspire and keep the populace at work, and these plus the usual transistor pop music that blared day and night meant that people could not sleep unless they collapsed from exhaustion.

More good news on the evening of Day Two was that the electricity in Government House was back on and that two out of the four elevators were working. Two would suffice for the Committee to go up and have a view from the roof terrace, as each elevator held twelve people. At Bomo Airport beer cans by the thousand had been swept away, tin and cardboard shacks razed, and the Control Building swept out, its windows either washed or remaining broken glass knocked out completely. The electricity in the Control Building did not work, and no plane had landed since the Committee's last visit years ago, except Bomo's private prop-driven plane which at the moment was out of order due to a missing part. His mechanics did not know what part it needed, so Bomo had ordered from America another prop plane which had not yet arrived.

Then during the night of Day Two one of the elevators got stuck with at least twenty men in it. The cleanup men and some soldiers had been celebrating the return of electricity with the ever abundant six-packs of beer, too many men had got into one elevator to take a ride, and the elevator had stopped between the third and fourth floors. Crowds of men and boys laughed and shouted advice all night:

'Keep pressing the buttons! Ha-ha!'

'Kick the door!'

'All of you push against one side!'

The men inside yelled that there wasn't enough air, and screamed for the elevator shaft to be shot open. There were sounds of anger and fighting within the elevator.

Boys banged the up and down buttons on all the floors until the buttons were smashed into the shaft panel or fell off it.

By dawn, the voices of the imprisoned men were hoarse. They were sweating to death, they said. Three of them, they said, were dead, and five others had fainted.

Bomo was awakened as soon as anybody dared to awaken him. What was to be done? Bomo dressed and walked to Government House scowling but looking very much in command. The mob in front and in the downstairs hall made way for him. On the ground floor, the elevator shaft with its closed door reminded him of some of the closed bank vaults he had seen in bank advertisements in Western magazines. He certainly did not want any damage done to

59

the front of that elevator shaft before the Committee arrived. Bomo mounted the stairs in his sandals, khaki trousers and shirt and a gold-braided cap for this emergency situation. At the height of the moans within the shaft, he paused and regarded the gold-coloured metal that surrounded the trapped elevator. How could anyone break that open, short of firing a cannon at it? Two hundred or more of his people on the stairway up and down stared at him expectantly, blankly, or sleepily. Wasting not a second in apparent hesitation, Bomo descended and the crowd parted to let him through.

'Electricians!' Bomo shouted.

Only one was pushed forth, a middle-aged man looking very scared. 'We think a safety device has stopped the elevator, because it was overcrowded, Your Excellency.'

Bomo lifted his cap and wiped a flood of sweat from his forehead. 'Is the electricity on? Is the air-conditioning working?'

'Yes, Your Excellency, but there is almost no ventilation in the elevator. The power is also weak.'

'Then close the goddam windows if the air-conditioning is on!' Bomo yelled. 'Goddammit, it's hotter than outside! – You've got the goddam *heat* on!'

It was true. In trying all the switches to get the elevator down, the cool air had been switched off and the heating on. When Bomo walked out on to Government House's front steps, the air was indeed cooler but also smoky. A chance wind blew a dark grey cloud of smoke straight across the façade of Government House and staggered Bomo, who turned and plunged into the building again with his hands over his face. Here he gave further orders as soon as he could breathe.

'Officers! Soldiers! Hurry up that garbage burning! *All* the burning! Burning got to finish by tomorrow night and the fires out!'

'Yes, Your Excellency!' said the nearest officer, and saluted before rallying his colleagues and plunging out of the door.

The electrician, a small man, was back at Bomo's elbow. 'Your Excellency, if we cannot lower the elevator by electrical power may we break in the outer structure in order to – '

'*No!*' Bomo yelled over the din of the yelping people in the foyer, more than half of whom were laughing. 'That elevator front is not to be broken!'

Bomo plunged down the steps again, yelling for a wet towel, wet with clean water. A couple of boys dashed through the haze to do his bidding. The street beyond was empty of cars that crept and cars that stood, and now only a few bicycles rolled along, and hand-drawn little wagons laden with trash, goods, buckets and jugs. From one of these, two wet cloths were obtained and brought back to Bomo who at once put one over his sweating head and face. The towel was someone's shirt, but no matter. People yelled and reeled, dodging the great wafts of smoke that cut the visibility to two metres at times. And the stench was awful, suggesting burnt meat, excrement and singed chicken feathers.

The next problem of the day was fire-fighting in a dozen or more places in the city. This meant water brigades, runners with buckets. Soldiers routed out all the idlers for this, and especially in demand were fleet-footed children. When Bomo got home to the Small Palace at nearly 2 p.m., exhausted, Lulu-Fey was practising her belly dance in the big living-room, and she complained about the smoke. Bomo told her that it couldn't be helped until they got all the cleaning up done.

The afternoon brought a cacophony of screams and rifle fire. Soldiers had been ordered to demolish the black markets which had openly displayed their Sony goods, porno items, tins of caviar and *foie gras*, and Jack Daniel's and Chivas Regal bottles, and the soldiers had met with armed resistance. Minor battles had started up, army machineguns had been brought into play, bottles confiscated and drunk.

And the evening brought further difficulties: more than half of the presumed twenty men in the trapped elevator had died or been killed in fistfights by the others. Their women were now clustered around the elevator shaft, attempting to break it open with hatchets. Bomo ordered the women removed or shot, both if necessary. Only a feeble moan or two came now from the elevator.

Bomo cursed the electricians. 'Let 'em die!' he yelled, not sure if anyone heard him.

They did die. By the end of the fifth day, no sound came from the elevator, but a smell did, a horrible smell of putrefaction, of something dead, not an unusual smell to Nabutians, but unusual coming from within the finest building of the land, Government House. Bomo asked for incense to be burnt, which unfortunately contributed a little to the infernal smoke which penetrated the building despite the fact that the windows were all supposed to be closed, and the air-conditioning running.

Not until the last minute, the evening of the day before the UN African Aid Committee was due to arrive in the morning at 11, did Bomo think of the limousines they would need at the airport. He gave his chauffeurs – twelve liveried men – hell for not having checked out the big Mercedes-Benzes days before now, but all the chauffeurs claimed to have been on their feet fighting fires. The Mercedes looked fine, but they would not run, not one of them, and Bomo had twenty. One needed a wheel and a carburettor, another a windshield, another a steering wheel, another the key even to open its doors, while other unstartable cars were a mystery. Bomo ordered his mechanics and chauffeurs to work all night, if necessary, and to get three limousines in working order.

They failed. It was Lulu-Fey's brilliant idea to have the citizenry pull the limousines by long gay cords. It would look more respectful, she remarked, and Bomo saw her point.

The UN Committee's small jet landed on schedule, but hit a couple of potholes in the runway, which knocked a wheel off and damaged one wing tip, so the Committee and its five aides disembarked in a state of slight shock.

Bomo's military band played the Nabutian national anthem. Children strewed flowers. Smoke still ringed the city, and some of the Committee members whipped out handkerchiefs to cover their noses and mouths after a few steps on land. Bomo advanced to meet them in his hottest uniform with the tunic collar and Sam Browne belt plus medals.

Douglas Hazelwood, head of the Committee, announced himself, smiled, and shook Bomo's hand warmly. So did all the others.

'Smoky!' someone remarked cheerfully.

Bomo had no reply, but kept his dignity as he led the way to five limousines in front of which barefoot children stood with long colourful cords and ropes in hand like horses champing at the bit. The smoke was a lot worse than at this time yesterday, because late last night, Bomo had made the mistake of ordering the fires put out with water, and many hadn't gone out entirely but were still smouldering. The usually blazing sun was only a hazy yellow patch in the grey sky, like the sun before a typhoon. Its heat came through but not its light, and the hour might have been dusk.

With the band marching behind, the limousines moved slowly toward the capital. The destination was the Hotel Bomo of Nabuti, where thirty-five rooms on the ground floor had been prepared.

Bomo had expected some wives and servants with the Committee. At any rate cold water ran in the hotel, even if there was no air-conditioning. This hotel was five storeys high, with elevators that did not work, but for the Committee's visit there was no need of elevators. Here the Committee unpacked, had a wash, and climbed back into the limousines, which had been waiting in the sun and smoke, to go to the Small Palace for an apéritif.

Lulu-Fey was dressed in a floor-length wrap-around cotton piece with gold bangles at wrists and ankles, feet bare. She made a charming hostess, Bomo thought with pride, even though she knew not a word of English. The gentlemen drank pink gins, Scotch and water, tomato juice, anything they wanted, while servants at all the windows and open doors swung decorative fans to keep out the smoke or at least stir it. Some of the Committee coughed, but all appeared merry and asked Bomo not too difficult questions about agriculture, copper, exports and health. They were to look at the copper mines later today, and since the mines were abandoned now Bomo had prepared a tale of worker unrest and strikes for wage increases so unreasonable that he had not yielded. Then, declining the limousines, they went off on foot toward Government House, because one of the Committee recalled from the last visit that it was within walking distance, though at the moment they couldn't see Government House for the smoke.

Roast pig. Olives. Baked yams and fresh fruit of all kinds, orange and purple flower blossoms, and fine silver. The long table with its white linen cloth looked rather splendid in the main salon, which was to the right of the elevators as one entered. But the smell was awful, and inexplicable. Bomo noticed the glances of puzzlement and alarm among the Committee before they sat down. And the smoke seemed to have followed them right into the salon. Champagne was poured by Bomo's best servants in white jackets and black trousers, then Bomo stood up and toasted his guests. He made a little speech of welcome and goodwill, which he had rehearsed only once, but the speech was none the worse for that. Bomo sounded sincere when he said: 'My country welcomes all of you and thanks you all for the many blessings, the machinery, the money you have given us.'

The guests applauded, coughed and smiled.

Lulu-Fey was on Bomo's left, smiling also, restless and eager for her part of the show which was her belly dance. Musicians sat in a corner playing on stringed instruments and a drum. Bomo saw to his annoyance that the windows had been opened and that servants worked to stir the haze of smoke as they had done in the Small Palace.

The roast pig and piglet had just been sliced and served, when there was an urgent knock on the closed hall door. When a servant opened the door, a man pitched forward on to the floor, and a billow of dark smoke followed him before the servant could get the door shut again. The fallen man's message was that the building seemed to be on fire. This was not at once translated into English, but the sudden alarm of the servants and of Bomo had everybody uneasy and several of the Committee got fearfully to their feet.

Bomo learned that some idiot had succeeded in pouring gasoline on the roof of the stuck elevator and dropping a match on to it, with an idea of cremating the bodies, which was the Nabutians' religious custom. A servant said a couple of the men's wives were responsible for this.

'*Gas masks!*' Bomo yelled. 'Get them fast – on pain of death!'

Servants scurried, soldier guards dashed about as if on fire themselves. Everyone had to get out, and everyone tried, though one Committee man collapsed on the floor and had to be dragged across the lobby. The elevator shaft leaked smoke at every invisible seam, like something about to explode, while the smell of the smoke suggested hellfire. Figures dashed or reeled out of the doors of Government House on to its steps, into a grey atmosphere in which objects were more visible but breathing hardly less dangerous.

'The gas masks, Your Excellency!' cried a lieutenant.

Soldiers rushed up with armloads of gas masks, which were opened and rapidly jammed on to the heads of the Committee members and their aides.

'Yo' moufs on d'*pipe*!' shouted Bomo, recalling suddenly some instructions he had heard long ago. He was pleased with his soldiers for having got the masks out so quickly. Along with his soldiers, a couple of whom already wore masks, Bomo helped buckle the masks securely around the necks of the dazed Committee men, and to lead them leftward toward the Small Palace, where the air appeared clearer, at least for the moment. Bomo gallantly declined a mask, and gripped Lulu-Fey protectively by the hand. Across her face she held a white napkin dampened with champagne.

The Committee staggered and struggled as if trying to get the masks off. Two men fell.

'Pick 'em up!' Bomo yelled to his soldiers.

Smoke swirled. A soldier with a mask dropped and lay writhing feebly.

In the Small Palace, servants got to work fanning. The Committee men were laid out on the floor, face up. Some didn't move. It was amazing to Bomo.

'More fans!' cried Bomo. 'And wet towels at once!' The towels were for the people without masks, like himself, for instance.

After a couple of minutes, things seemed to be better. The wind had shifted in their favour, fresher air blew through the house. But of the gentlemen of the Committee and their aides only two or three stirred and were still again, moaning.

Kuo, who had left his tour of duty to attend the banquet, waved smoke from before his face, rubbed his eyes, and said, 'We might take their masks off now, father. Y'think?' He was stooped on his heels like Bomo, not to see the men on the floor better, but because the smoke tended to rise in the room.

Bomo agreed. He and Kuo and a couple of servants began unbuckling the masks. One servant cried out in alarm, shrilly, though it was a man servant.

'*Ants!*' he yelled in his native tongue, shaking both hands.

'Holy spirits! You are right!' Kuo jumped up, slapping his hands together, rubbing their backs. 'Them big grey ants!'

Everyone knew this particular grey ant, which hibernated or aestivated in the oddest places, and emerged in droves, bloodthirsty and furious, if disturbed. They had got into the filter fronts of the masks, a circular flat portion that was porous but rather felt-like. Now all hands in the house fell to dragging the Committee men by the shoulders or feet out of the house, because it would be hell indeed if several of these ants escaped and stayed in the house. The idea was to remove the masks and burn them outdoors. Kuo, with white gloves on now, got the first mask off and found the man's face bleeding from ant bites besides being blue. Servants hopped, masks were cut off, and Bomo ordered a fire started on the Small Palace lawn.

Shrieks came again, from servants male and female. Napkins, towels, anything to wipe the infuriated ants from forearms, hands and bare feet! Every man whose mask was removed was blue-faced, dead from asphyxiation, because the ants' bodies had blocked the air flow through the filters from the start.

Ghastly as it was, Bomo had to give orders for all twenty corpses to be burnt. Their bodies were arranged in a ring with feet outermost like the spokes of a wheel. No time for niceties! The ants had to be dealt with first, so kerosene was poured over the masks and heads, a match thrown.

Servants stamped the ground, looking for fleeing ants. Squealing as ants nipped her bare feet, Lulu-Fey shot spray from a can of insecticide which she had found in the Small Palace's kitchen, making a circle with it on the ground around the projecting legs of the Committee men and their aides.

'The pilot!' Bomo said suddenly, frowning, recalling that he had seen one figure at the controls of the plane, maybe two.

His son Kuo heard him, and raised a finger to indicate that he understood. 'I send a message to the airport!' He spoke with one of his soldiers who stood nearby tending the fire, and drew a finger across his own throat, and the soldier departed.

The American pilot and co-pilot, who had stayed behind at the airport to try to repair, with the help of some Nabutians, the damage done to their small jet, were surprised by a squad of five soldiers with bayonets on their rifles, who approached them in an aggressive manner and beheaded them without a word.

So disappeared the United Nations Committee on African Aid, which was a division of – some other well-meaning department. The small jet had its useful contents removed, also its motor, and the carcass was broken up and burnt beyond recognition the evening of the same day as the deaths of its passengers. When the telephone calls came in the next day, asking where Mr Hazelwood and his Committee were, the telephone operator, on Bomo's orders, said that the Committee's plane had never arrived, though they had been expecting it yesterday morning at 11. It was easy to suggest that their neighbour country Gibbi, which was known to be always making trouble for Nabuti, had shot the plane down. At any rate, President Bomo had no information to give, and deeply regretted that the Committee had not been able to make its visit, to which he had been so much looking forward.

SWEET FREEDOM! AND A PICNIC ON THE WHITE HOUSE LAWN

You bump into them everywhere, in New York, in Chicago or Philadelphia, or they bump into you. They are called nuts, if the citizens are in a tolerant mood, and parasites if the citizens are not. They are mildly or totally insane, often ranting to the open sky, or earnestly conversing with someone who is not there.

Nobody knows what to do with them. 'There're so many of them!' some people say in desperation. Or 'Why do they all have to come to New York?' Or Chicago, or wherever. There are as many females as males, sometimes hard to tell which, since the garb is an overcoat, worn-out flat shoes or boots, an old felt hat or a pulled down woollen cap, and they don't bother with haircuts. They gravitate to big cities, because there they can be anonymous, they don't stand out like sore thumbs, they can sleep in doorways, go underground and live in the subways for a few days, or in winter find a warm grille in the pavement and stake it out, defend it from would-be usurpers and sharers by interlacing barbed wire in the grille except for the length needed for one person to sleep on. In big cities there are also doss houses costing from one to three dollars a night, but there one has to watch out for thieves among fellow-sleepers.

Where do they come from? Many are from state mental institutions, released with instructions to go to the nearest drug dispensary and get the pills needed. 'It won't cost you anything, but don't lose your prescription or the address of the dispensary.' Many of these people are too far gone to hang on to anything, or to remember that they are supposed to take pills once a day or week. No matter, the overcrowded institutions were shot of them. Still other of these wandering zombie-like figures are castouts of ordinary households. Old Aunt Fran, who could never get along with anybody, because she suspected and kept accusing everybody of plotting against her, a belief confirmed to her when her own family pushed her out of the house. Or Cousin Ben, a bachelor and inclined to tipple, a habit which cost him his job, and now he wanders the streets of New York, reduced to cheap wine from the Scotch for which he once had a fine palate.

Aline Schroeder, going out of her kitchen door to hang some laundry on the line, was surprised to see two strange men standing in her garden, apparently absorbed in looking at the roses. Having set her basket down, she was approaching them to ask what they wanted, when they turned toward her, and she screamed.

'Eddie! – Eddie, come *down*!' And she ran toward the house. Aline Schroeder knew mental cases when she saw them.

That was a Thursday morning in a small town in Ohio. Eddie Schroeder, getting nothing from the two vague men, except that one wanted to go to Chicago and the other to New York, kept an eye on them, while he asked his wife to telephone the police.

'They've escaped from the loony bin,' Eddie murmured to her. 'I don't want to take 'em on. Not our business.'

'They were supposed to go to the bus stop,' said the police when they arrived. 'Brookfield's letting a hundred or so go back home today. These two must've just wandered off.' The police, with no trouble, got the men into their car with a promise to take them to the town bus terminal.

Aline Schroeder was speechless with shock, and Eddie was scowling.

'Get 'em all the hell outa *here*, Sam,' Eddie said to one cop, whom he knew.

'We will, but we got strict orders to treat 'em kindly,' the officer replied.

Aline Schroeder went into her kitchen and made herself a cup of tea. The story got round town, of course. And, despite the police efforts, the residents of Temple are not yet convinced that the police got them all out of town that memorable Thursday. Especially since more, many more 'official medical discharges' occurred since. Yet the old Brookfield Center edifice on the edge of town is still overcrowded.

Brookfield Center is typical of many state and semi-state-run institutions in the United States. It is occupied not entirely by the mentally ill, because it accepts also the elderly whose families haven't the money for more expensive rest homes, and also convalescent people from state hospitals. Nevertheless in Temple, Ohio, Brookfield has always been known as 'the loony bin'. It was common knowledge that some rooms had padded walls and windows with bars. One could see these windows from the outside. Residents of Temple fifty and sixty years old could remember driving past Brookfield with their parents when they were children, and staring at the windows, hoping to see the face of an inmate, though at the same time scared too, because even then it was 'the loony bin'. Parents discouraged the children's curiosity, suggesting that the inmates were all dangerous people, though also to be pitied. But one thing was certain, they had to be kept locked up.

Because of overcrowding in such institutions, a directive went out from Washington, D C in the late 1960s, and was repeated in the 1970s, to release inmates who were not considered violent. This came as a blessing to Brookfield's harassed staff and to many other such places across the nation. The same message went to prisons, and the slogan was 'economy plus humanity', meaning that the nation could save money by doing this, as well as make life happier for people whose confinement was not necessary.

Some ten percent of Brookfield Center inmates sprang to the minds of Dr Nelson and his head nurse, Superintendent Dorothy Sweeney, when they received their 'Guidance Paper on Federal and State Medical and Psychiatric Institutions', faces they knew well, along with many of their names too.

'Louis Jones,' said Superintendent Sweeney. 'God knows he's harmless. Takes his sedatives by himself now.' And she smiled her first smile in months.

'Ye-es,' said Dr Nelson, thinking that Louis Jones was innocence itself after a decade of sedatives. Louis was simply vague, a bit sleepy-looking. 'And Miss Tiller, maybe.'

'Yes, and the Kelly twins maybe. And Bert! – And Claude! We must make a list. Then we'll look at our records and add a lot more.'

They made a list. Nothing wrong with Miss Tiller, except that she thought she was Cleopatra, and hadn't she a relative in Massachusetts with whom she might stay, at first, at least? Nothing wrong with Bert, who was the soul of politeness. And of course Brookfield would arrange to keep in touch with all these people. What a relief it would be to have some breathing space in Brookfield!

When Dr Nelson and Superintendent Sweeney broke the news that evening in the refectory during dinner and over the loudspeaker, not everyone understood, which was to be expected.

'Some of you will be leaving soon – *if* you want to go. And when and if it is convenient for all concerned.' Superintendent Sweeney said with a smile. Five or six strong male helpers stood, as usual, around the walls of the refectory, hands free in case of trouble.

But few heads looked up from the soup bowls. Miss Tiller, who surely would have had a rejoinder, as she had for every Brookfield announcement or regulation, was not present, because she insisted on her meals being served in her room, where she ignored the three women who shared the room with her, unless it was to give them orders, which they in turn ignored.

'Nothing to worry about!' Superintendent Sweeney continued cheerfully. 'Just the opposite! So this should be an especially happy dinner time!'

'Who's leaving?' a creaky voice asked.

'Leaving where?' asked a woman.

'Where? . . . Who? . . . *Where?*'

More than half the assembled diners, however, might not have heard the announcement. The Brookfield Center staff had decided that it was better to give advance notice like this, and to let it sink into the minds of a few, than to have certain well-known faces vanish from the scene, and also to prevent the releasees from feeling that they were suddenly being ousted. The staff had foreseen that some might resist going, whereas some not fit to leave might want to.

This was more or less the picture, when Superintendent Sweeney, a younger nurse, and a couple of male helpers set about informing individuals, and helping them pack up. Sweeney was convinced that some were suddenly pretending helplessness, confusion or whatever, because Brookfield had been a comfortable berth for just too long. Her temper came back, and she said to more than one: 'You *are* going, whether you like it or not, because there're plenty that need this room more than you do!'

Miss Gloria Tiller professed to be 'utterly delighted' at the prospect of leaving this curious and ill-kept palace, and said she expected her barge at the door the following morning.

Meanwhile, the same thing was happening at prisons. The quiet types, the alert and often jocular types, ageing rapists who had been in the jug for decades, myriads of petty thieves, one- and two-time muggers, tranquil-looking murderers of low IQ who had spent the past years learning shoe repair and plumbing – thousands of these were set free from Maine to California.

They took buses, they hitchhiked, some had friends or relatives who wired airfares, many simply walked. All were given between fifty and a hundred dollars in cash, depending on the wealth of the State, 'to enable them to get to their families or to other destinations'.

A taciturn and pleasant-looking man of fifty, who had been in prison for the past thirteen years for 'repeated rape', saw his sexual fantasy materialise hardly ten minutes after he quit a penal institution in Illinois. A girl in a bright summer dress was riding a bicycle toward him, pedalling in a leisurely way along the sunlit road at whose edge the released man, one Fred Wechsler, had been trying to hitch a ride to somewhere. Fred did not hesitate. He threw himself in front of the bicycle, which rolled over him, bouncing the girl off, and he satisfied his desire in a ditch conveniently near. His dream had come true! Freedom was heaven, heaven again! Fred climbed out of the ditch and walked on, having remembered to pick up his carryall with his few possessions. Soon he got a ride southward. The girl in the ditch had been knocked out by her fall, but realised what had happened when she came to. She reported this mishap to the police in her small town.

In Raleigh, North Carolina, expert car thieves who had not met in prison made acquaintance in a café near the penitentiary from which they had just been released, and decided to pool their talents.

But for many of the mentally ill, freedom struck them like a fog, and they didn't know where to go.

Letters began to come in from the public to newspapers and radio stations. Newspaper items lent credence to the public's anxiety: a man who had suffered bankruptcy, then a breakdown and 'loss of mental competence', made his way back to the headquarters of his former company which had the same name but was in other hands, and insisted that he was still its head, and that the crooks should get out. He put up a fight, when an attempt was made to eject him, grabbed a fire axe, killed a woman and wounded two men before he could be subdued. In another incident, a divorced woman returned to her old home, where her former husband lived with his new wife and family, and refused to leave, the 'authorities' had to be called in, and the woman taken away forcibly, leaving the family in a state of shock.

Miss Tiller, alias Cleopatra, had declined to take the bus laid on by Brookfield Center, preferring to wait for her barge, for which she looked anxiously along the highway. She was joined by a courteous man of short stature, whose gestures indicated that he wished to be of assistance, and Miss Tiller handed him a reticule containing her nightdress, two long gowns, and her make-up kit. She hailed a huge dark shape coming toward them on the highway, hailed it so urgently and with such determination that the shape stopped.

It was an eighteen-wheel truck, two men sat up in the driver's cabin, and one got down. Miss Tiller and the helpful little man climbed aboard.

'Where y'bound?' asked the driver.

'Alexandria,' replied Miss Tiller.

'Y'mean – what State d'y'mean? Virginia?'

'State? Egypt!' said Miss Tiller.

Bert nodded accord with Miss Tiller.

'No kiddin'!' said the driver, genuinely surprised.

'You'll be wantin' the airport then. Cleveland, maybe.' The man next to the driver had begun to smile. 'We're headin' in the wrong direction for the airport.'

Miss Tiller turned her narrow and rather elegant face to him and said, 'I'll be going by barge, thank you.'

The driver laughed, and started moving. 'Barge! – By canal maybe?'

They drove through the little town of Temple, where Miss Tiller said she did not want to be put down, but she grew excited at the sight of the next town which was much larger, and she told the driver he could let her down anywhere. It was the presence of so many people that excited her.

Bert got down with her.

Miss Tiller rose on her toes and sniffed the air like a hunting dog. 'This is more like it!'

Bert plucked at the front of his Brookfield-issue shirt, as if it disgusted him, and glanced up at Miss Tiller.

'Clothes!' she said, knowing Bert didn't hear her, because she had realised by now that he was a deaf-mute.

The first department store they entered had clothes not to the taste of either, and Bert indicated with grimaces that he thought the prices outrageous, while Miss Tiller informed a shopgirl that she wouldn't have any of the items as a gift. In another street they came upon a thrift shop whose window held all manner of interesting garments. Bert at once bought a black derby, trousers, a pair of big comfortable shoes, and a jacket, all of which cost hardly twenty dollars, and he acquired a cane for fifty cents. Miss Tiller took somewhat longer for her purchases, but found what she wanted, a long purple dress with gold sequins and a terrible rent down the back, unfortunately, but she was so slender the material could overlap, and with a broad red alligator belt, the rent did not show. She bought high-heeled sandals – such a pleasure after the medium-heeled shoes issued by Brookfield that were neither here nor there – and a large flat purse into which she put her money, make-up and comb.

'My servant will pay,' she said as she started to walk out of the door. She was stopped.

Bert paid gallantly for both of them, whereupon Miss Tiller handed over all her money, eighty dollars, into Bert's care.

'Royalty does not carry money,' said Miss Tiller.

They went in search of an eating place, and were attracted by a gold-painted diner from which cheerful music came. Lots of heads turned as they walked in, for Miss Tiller wore a rhinestone tiara now.

'Hey, who's *she?*' a man asked.

'Look, it's Charlie Chaplin!' a little boy yelled.

'Cleopatra, Queen of all Egypt,' Miss Tiller replied, when asked by two workmen in overalls who she was.

Meanwhile, Bert did a few turns to the music whose beat he could detect by throbs in the floor and his eardrums, dancing around his cane, and smiling at the people in booths and on stools. Miss Tiller had lent him some black mascara at his request, and he had given himself a moustache and arched eyebrows.

People stared and clapped. Even the waitresses were fascinated.

'Can you dance? Give us a dance!' someone said.

The jukebox was playing a waltz. Bert gracefully extended his hand, and Miss Tiller put down her hamburger.

Bert had no bill to pay at that diner, and in fact he had collected fourteen dollars or more in bills and coins from the floor, when they departed to applause.

'You two come back 'n' see us!' a waitress said.

Two days after being released from prison, the man who liked girls on bicycles had raped five more, and was now in another State. He had bought a change of clothing with his discharge money, and he spent some on food, but so far nothing on transport or housing as the weather was mild. He got lifts easily along the highways, and he didn't care at all in which direction he went.

BIKE-GIRL RAPER HITS NINTH VICTIM!

a headline said by the time Fred Wechsler got to Oklahoma. The nation knew what he looked like from victims' descriptions: about fifty, five feet eight or nine, greying brown hair, clean shaven, grey or light-blue eyes, medium build. The trouble was that several million men could match this portrait.

Different shocks were occurring on the West Coast, where prisons and hospitals for mental cases had emptied themselves of all inmates who had good conduct records. The climate was mild, and parking lots and shopping malls were now graced with sleeping forms, groups playing cards by candlelight or torchlight, some singing and drinking wine. Adolescent boys made a sport of harassing these people and got rid of at least three by throwing them over a cliff in the direction of the Pacific. Dwellers in some regions began staying home after nightfall, not wanting to wreck their cars or injure themselves by running over a sleeper on the street, or to be accosted by beggars, or worse, mugged. Bars and discos, cinemas and even restaurants began to lose money, and were consequently behind the Troll-Bashers, as the adolescent cleanup boys called themselves. These boys forcibly removed many people from the streets, took them in pick-up trucks beyond the city limits, and dumped them.

The government was blamed, the prisons and loony bins were blamed. There was a war between the government and the media, the government trying to minimise the seriousness of the problem ('Lots of people prefer to sleep outdoors,' said the President), and the media wanting to get all the facts and to show interesting pictures on television. Some typical newspaper and TV items were:

UNKNOWN TENOR TAKES THE STAGE AT THE MET

A man rushed on to the stage during a performance of Puccini's *Tosca* Friday night, pushed Mario aside, and took the hero's part rather well in a duet with the leading lady, who was understandably in a quandary as to what to do. Laughter gave way to amazement at the quality of the intruder's performance. He was identified as George Jennings, 26, former inmate of a hospital in North Carolina.

and

Shoppers in New York were surprised to see a plump, elderly man sitting on the sidewalk outside a department store, clad only in a white tablecloth tied about himself like a diaper. He professed, in baby talk, to have been abandoned by his mother . . .

Then there were stories of people who walked on all fours, and, while some newspaper readers wrote letters accusing journalists of inventing these stories, other readers sent photographs of people walking in this manner in their towns. One woman in Kansas wrote an open letter to the President, which her town newspaper printed:

For the past six months, I have been plagued by a man who thinks my house is his boyhood home, and that I am a certain relative who has usurped the house from him. I am sick and tired of finding this sleeping hulk against my front door when I open it to get the morning paper. The police have twice removed him, but within days he is back. I beg of you to put this man and people like him back where they belong!

The raper of girls on bikes had acquired a bike himself, and got to Mississippi, then Louisiana, where the weather was still clement. His health had improved, and he picked up money here and there doing odd jobs such as lawn-mowing and yard-tidying, for which he proposed such a low price per hour that few people said no. He made a good impression. Not a soul suspected that he was the rapist sought from coast to coast. A pretty girl in a family did not excite him at all. Only a girl rolling along on a bike turned him on, and by sheer luck, he had so far encountered such a sight only on roads rather far from houses and other people. He could not have counted his conquests by now, and it did not interest him to count them, but the police and the newspapers did, and his score was twenty-eight. Police were tracking him southward, and were once within twenty miles of him, by now looking for a man on a bike, but Fred Wechsler, who did not read newspapers, bought himself a second-hand car around this time. Long ago, before he had been sent to prison, he had driven a car, and the dealer did not ask to see his driving licence.

'A major national and societal tragedy,' the American Psychiatric Society said in commenting on the practice of discharging the still

75

mentally ill from state institutions. 'Hardly a section of the country has escaped the ubiquitous presence of these ill and hallucinating human beings, wandering our city streets, huddling in alleys, sleeping over vents. Such is the result of Washington's shameful policy of cutting federal spending . . .'

The President replied that the majority of those released had relatives, that charity begins at home, and that Americans had a tradition of giving voluntary aid to the sick and homeless. 'In America, people can make it if they try. That's what America is all about.' This became known as the 'Bowl of Soup' speech. A woman wrote a letter which was printed in *Time*:

> The law-makers and the federal funds distributors in their luxurious quarters in Washington, DC do not see what we see on our streets and doorsteps. I suggest that we citizens band together and bus these criminals and zombies to the White House and show them what we're talking about.
>
> (Mrs) Mary V. Benson
> Tallahassee, Florida

This letter was to have important repercussions.

Miss Tiller and Bert had not been without a roof over their heads since their first day of freedom. On their first evening, thinking to treat themselves to a steak dinner, they had entered a roadside restaurant called The Steak Place, where there was a pianist beside the bar. The diners could ask the pianist to play songs of their choice. Miss Tiller found this civilised. Bert whistled a tune to the pianist, who at once began playing 'Who Will Come and Buy My Violets?', a background song for one of Charlie Chaplin's most famous films. Seeing Bert in his Chaplin gear, the people at the tables gave a patter of applause, and there were cries of 'Dance for us! . . . Give us a waltz!'

Miss Tiller conveyed the request to Bert by opening her arms, and waltzing by herself, while Bert twirled gracefully on one foot, the other foot extended in the air behind him. He leaned pensively on his cane, waltzed some shy steps with Miss Tiller, who was taller than he, created his dance as he went along, while Miss Tiller seemed just out of reach, in two senses, to him.

'More! . . . More!'

The pianist began another waltz from the old days, Irving Berlin's

'All Alone', and Bert and Miss Tiller took the dance floor, where a spot was thrown on them, and their appearance provoked shouts of delight. Miss Tiller waltzed and sang, pretending to hold a telephone in her hands.

A money bowl sat on the piano but, for Bert and Miss Tiller, patrons approached and poked bills into Bert's jacket pockets and into Miss Tiller's purse, which hung by its strap over her arm, and which she graciously opened. Others sailed bills folded like aeroplanes on to the dance floor, and from time to time Bert zoomed his cane under them, or bent from the waist to pick them up, causing Miss Tiller to bump him once and knock him flat.

The manager spoke with them, when they returned to their table, or rather he spoke with Miss Tiller. Would they agree to come back for the next two nights, Friday and Saturday? Could Miss Tiller sing again? Yes, of course she could. Half-hour shows at 9 and 11:30 p.m., one hundred dollars per evening, plus what the customers gave, the hotel expenses included? The manager owned a hotel fifty yards away.

Miss Tiller replied that she thought the proposition most interesting. Bert, watching, nodded his assent. The manager was a little puzzled when Miss Tiller signed an informal agreement with 'Cleopatra', but he said nothing. He was not surprised when Bert signed 'Charlie Chaplin'.

Miss Tiller's voice was reedy on the high notes, and some she couldn't touch at all, such as a few in Strauss's Zerbinetta aria, for instance, but nobody cared. Now she had her barge. Three armless upholstered chairs made it with a couple of long curtains thrown over them, a waiter rolled her on stage, she smoking a cigarette in a long holder. Miss Tiller plainly enjoyed her performances, enjoyed even the laughter at her bad notes. Something magical, something happy flowed between her and Bert, and between them both and the audience. They had to consult with each other like amateurs between numbers, and before informing the pianist what to play. People wanted to shake their hands after a show. And the money fell like rain.

The owner of The Steak Place, whose restaurant was packed on Saturday night, could not match the money offered Miss Tiller and Bert by a couple of entrepreneurs from San Francisco. Miss Tiller and Bert were off and away.

Mrs Mary V. Benson had struck a common chord with her letter in *Time*. More letters were printed in *Time* on the subject, and letters came in to Mrs Benson in Tallahassee. *Yes, let's show Washington!* was the idea. They organised. This took weeks, but voluntary effort, which the President had advocated, was not lacking for this cause: gather up the zombies, the panhandlers, the nuts, the exhibitionists, and send them to the White House lawn. Bus companies got into the spirit and offered free transport. Washington, getting wind of this, decided to adopt a 'Welcome to All Comers' attitude, and promised a picnic and an open-air forum where people could exchange views, even with the President himself.

The day was set, April 17th, a Wednesday. Trains and buses, even airlines offered free tickets for the publicity it gave them, and many people who had cars took drifters in their towns to the nearest bus terminal or airport. The White House had expected a few thousand, perhaps five thousand, and intended to deploy plain-clothes guards as well as the National Guard and the police to keep the crowds in order. But Washington, D C had had only some twelve hours' notice that fifty to sixty thousand would probably arrive.

To make matters worse, it was raining. Tent-like roofs were put up over the long tables of sandwiches and soft drinks on the White House lawns, but a couple of tents collapsed before noon, causing panic among the men and women caught underneath. Many thought they had been invited to live in the White House, and were angry at learning, after having come all this way, that all that was being offered them was cold food and iced tea out in the rain. Hundreds began drifting toward the White House – where was the President, after all? – and, when the guards took a stand against them, fights broke out, bullets rubber and real began to fly. The National Guard lost its temper, and bashed some heads with rifle butts. Helicopters dropped armed reinforcements by rope ladder close to the White House, and these descended on to the heads of people.

Meanwhile yet more were arriving by bus or on foot, because of the congestion of vehicles and troop carriers.

'Let us in our home!' some shouted, and this became a chant.

There were screams, female and male, as people were trampled.

Helicopters and White House door guards released tear gas bombs, with an idea of driving the horde away from the White House but, due to the wind, the gas affected the troops as much as anyone else. Then the White House doors yielded. All this was seen on TV across the nation, and viewers yelled, 'Look! – *Good!*' or 'How horrible!' or merely laughed wildly, depending on their turn of mind.

The tear gas, invisible but smarting to the eyes, seemed merely to animate the masses on the wet lawns. Machinegun fire came from within the White House. A TV news helicopter collided with a military helicopter and both fell on the crowd, but did not burst into flame.

'Welcome – welcome – and be calm, please!' the President's voice said for at least the fourth time on a recorded message boomed out from the White House balcony, where only armed soldiers stood ready to fire. The President at that moment was hiding in a steel vault in the White House basement. The vault was specially made for such an emergency, with inside controls for opening, and food and water for two or three people for a week. He had been hidden away like a Queen Bee in the centre of her hive, and a hive it was with derelicts, the mentally deranged, the half-blinded from tear gas, creeping up and down the fine staircases, opening the doors to every room. Despite the flying bullets and the falling figures, more pushed through the main doors.

The National Guard and the Marines, having shot up all their ammunition, became scared for the good reason that they were outnumbered and seemed to be fighting suicidal masses. They were now using their rifles as battering rams against the people and as staves to defend themselves. TV crews in their helicopters overhead were filming, reporting: 'It looks like a battlefield here! The fallen – the fallen are mostly around the White House front porch, but – Yes! More National Guards are coming up from the *streets* now, trying to push forward and steer people off the lawn. We've never seen anything – anything like it, not even the hunger march in the Hoover Administration – surely! . . .'

The White House lawn activities, when they became rough between 2 and 3 p.m., interrupted an after-lunch show that Miss Tiller and Bert were giving in a large Boston hotel. In a way, the laughter that these two had started continued, as the people at the tables were treated to a big-screen TV viewing.

'These are the – the – ' yelled the emcee, at a loss for words.

'The *loonies!*' someone supplied, and there was loud laughter, because the march today to Washington had been well publicised.

'The Moonies, the zombies, the muggers – '

'Let's *hope*!' cried a woman.

'At least they won't be hanging around our neighbourhoods tonight!'

'Yee-*hoo*!' Applause!

'Where's the President in all this?'

'Bet he's hiding in the wine cellar!' someone yelled back.

Miss Tiller and Bert were equally rapt, eyes on the big screen.

'Isn't it shocking!' Miss Tiller said to Bert, despite the fact that he couldn't hear her. 'People behaving like that! The rabble! – They consider themselves unemployed, I suppose. What this country needs is slaves!' Her voice rose as she realised that she wished to address her audience, which happened to be a real estate dealers' convention. She stepped into the centre of the floor, and the spot man put the light on her. She said in a loud and elegant voice: 'Look at that rabble! What this country needs is *slaves* – as in *my* country – Egypt! This could never happen in Egypt! – I'd put them to work building *pyramids*!'

Loud hand-clapping and laughter! 'Yee-hoo-o! You tell 'em, Cleo!'

Miss Tiller now wore an asp partly in and partly out of the top of her gown at her somewhat flat bosom. The asp was of rubbery plastic, but very lifelike, moving its head about with Miss Tiller's movements.

The restaurant patrons did not realise how serious Miss Tiller was in her remark about slaves.

Slaves, real slaves might be out of the question just now, Miss Tiller thought, America wasn't ready for them yet, but she had no complaint about the services she enjoyed. She and Bert now had a manager, whom Miss Tiller preferred to call their Public Relations Officer, a young man of twenty-eight whom they had met in San Francisco on their first trip. Miss Tiller had pulled him into line once, she was good at figures and kept an eye on the books, and maybe Harvey Knowles – that was his name – had made an honest mistake, but in future he was not going to make any more mistakes, honest or not. They had played in Chicago, Dallas and New Orleans. She and Bert stayed in good hotels, which made an impression upon journalists, and Bert wanted to be near her because of his communication problem, so they always took a suite. Miss Tiller was now doing impersonations, Gloria Swanson, for example, Garbo. She loved to pretend to be someone else, loved to act self-assured, and in fact she was, with no worries at all about her future or that of her devoted Bert.

Miss Tiller and Bert had not connected the surging, milling crowds on the White House lawn with any people they had ever known. They had both entered a new and better world in the past months. Miss Tiller had much expanded her repertory, while Bert had invented pantomime skits with real little stories to them, some involving Miss Tiller and some not. Bert's props were a bouquet of flowers, sometimes an ashcan, an imaginary window toward which he directed his attention while he danced and mimed. They were going to England soon with a six-week contract starting in Manchester and ending in London.

In the next days, the President cluck-clucked over the White House mishap, which had cost nearly five hundred lives. The President sombrely stated that the government would do all in its power to house those homeless and 'mentally challenged' individuals, but that it was up to their families and their communities to lend a hand too. 'There but for the grace of God go I – and you and you,' the President intoned with sad and thoughtful mien.

The left-wing press suggested that the right-wing government was delighted at having eliminated half a thousand of what it considered undesirables, and to have terrorised thousands more. A story about the President hiding in a vault in the White House basement was bandied about, some swearing it was true, but unlike the people-walking-on-all-fours story, no one had photographed the President in the vault, so it became a joke that just might be true.

'I bet a couple of thousand got killed,' said a Washington, DC resident. 'I heard a lot of machinegun fire. No mistake!'

Fred Wechsler, the raper, saw some of the Washington, DC uproar on the TV in his motel room in Florida, and shook his head. Those people just didn't know how to live, hadn't adjusted to freedom. Fred had raped a girl of about thirteen that day. Now he was eating a sandwich in comfort and security, he had a roof over his head and a car. He recalled some of his friends in the Illinois prison where he had spent thirteen years, one called Willy Armstrong, in for breaking and entering, a nice fellow but simple-minded, easily led astray, and Fred wondered if Willy had been dumb enough to go to that phoney picnic on the White House lawn and get shot?

TROUBLE AT THE JADE TOWERS

'Live – in luxury and security at the Jade Towers,' said the discreet advertisements for the posh eighty-eight-storey apartment building on Lexington Avenue in the 1970s. The stone-floored lobby, the elevators and the corridors were all of the same light green, the most restful of colours. The entrance doors of bullet-proof glass could be opened only by doormen who stood between the first pair of glass doors and the second which gave on to the lobby. On the ground floor, there was a small beauty parlour and a barber shop, a florist's, a coffee shop, a cosy piano bar, a tiny but elegant delicatessen, and an automatised post office, all for resident patronage. Philodendrons and rubber plants almost hid the entrances to these little service spots. On the eighty-seventh floor, below the penthouse apartments, was a heated swimming pool lined with jade-coloured tiles. On the roof, twin towers with domed tops of light green hue suggested ageing copper, yet unmistakably marked the Jade Towers, which rapidly became the finest place to live, if you could afford it.

And people came, signed leases or bought apartments. Would-be buyers and renters were screened, and a famous female pop singer and an Atlantic City casino owner got turned away, facts which were reported in *People* magazine and gossip columns of some New York newspapers.

Near the end of the Jade Towers' first five months, the management was able to boast that there had been no house robbery, no mugging, no violence of any kind on its premises, and the building was now ninety-five percent occupied.

Sidney Clark, the day-shift manager at the reception desk, was quite surprised one morning, when a tenant in apartment 3 M telephoned down to complain about cockroaches in her kitchen. She had seen two, she said.

'We just moved in yesterday, and I haven't even bought a loaf of bread as yet,' the woman said. 'I did bring in some tonic water and a container of milk this morning, but they're not even opened.'

'We'll look into it at once, Mrs Fenton, and I *am* sorry,' said Mr Clark.

'Finlay. I'm shocked, because everything's so new and clean in the building.'

The desk manager smiled. 'Yes, Mrs Finlay, and we'll keep it that way. I'll report this to our exterminator, and he'll look in some time today, certainly tomorrow. We'll telephone you first and won't enter the apartment unless you're there.'

Sidney Clark had a second cockroach complaint an hour later from a couple on the tenth floor. He had already called up Ex-Pest, the exterminating firm with which the Jade Towers had contracted, Ex-Pest was coming that afternoon, and he made a note of the tenth-floor apartment. Then he decided to visit the Jade Cup, the coffee shop in one of the two side galleries on the ground floor. Its jade floor and counter looked shiny and clean, with not a crumb in sight. He told the woman manager about the two cockroach complaints, and asked to have a look at the kitchen. The kitchen looked as clean as the counter and tables, apart from the slight disorder normal for kitchens. Mr Clark stared at the wrapped and unwrapped loaves of bread, at the danish pastries.

'Odd to have two complaints in one day,' he said to the manageress who had accompanied him.

'Oh, cockroaches,' the middle-aged woman replied, wrinkling her nose with distaste. 'Can't do much about 'em, you know, even in the best of buildings. Wherever there's people and water, let alone kitchens, there's roaches no matter how clean you are.'

Mr Clark gave her a grim smile. 'Well, not in the Jade Towers, Miss – '

'Mrs Donleavy.'

'Mrs Donleavy. The Jade Towers has got to be perfect and stay perfect, because we've filled this building on a promise of perfection. So I'll expect you to keep your end up by seeing that the Jade Cup is immaculate.'

'Do you see anything wrong now, sir? – And I haven't seen a cockroach down here, not one,' said Mrs Donleavy.

'Let me know right away if you do,' said Mr Clark, departing.

Two Ex-Pest men came around 4 that afternoon, and visited the two apartments from which there had been complaints. Ex-Pest reported to Mr Clark an hour or so later that they hadn't seen any cockroaches in the two kitchens in question, but that they had fumigated both kitchens, and advised the tenants to keep the kitchen doors closed for an hour.

'We're using a new agent, Ex-Pest Unique, practically odourless. Our own labs made it and we've got a patent on it. Here – I'll leave you this.' With a smile, the reddish-haired Ex-Pest man, in dark green cap and work uniform, laid a brochure on the chest-high reception desk top, and gave it a slap.

'Thank you,' said Mr Clark, annoyed that the Ex-Pest men had entered the lobby from the rear service elevator, each with Ex-Pest embroidered in white on the left pocket of his dark green shirt. 'Would you leave by the back entrance, please?'

'Oh, sure,' said the smiling man, with a cheery wave.

A couple in rather fancy dress were entering the lobby at that moment. Mr Clark knew that Hiram Zilling, a wealthy Texan, was giving a cocktail party starting at 6 p.m. in his penthouse apartment. Mr Clark directed the couple to the proper elevator, an express for the penthouses.

In the next days, Mr Clark was the recipient of a few compliments, which he courteously acknowledged and promised to pass on to 'the management'. The swimming pool was a great success, eliciting some verbal and one written word of praise. It had a raised and sloping middle section, where bathers could lie and 'sun' at any time during the day or night under invisible sunlamps which directed their tanning rays downward. This feature was listed among the Jade Towers' many 'time-savers' in its advertisements, along with the day and night post office with photocopying machines and computers that gave information on air transport including prices, and enabled people to buy tickets with credit cards.

Mr Clark, after ten days, thought the cockroaches a thing of the past, when he suddenly had three complaints in one day. These were from apartments on floors seven, eight and fourteen, which was actually thirteen, Mr Clark always recalled, rather to his annoyance, because he disliked cluttering his brain with unimportant side-thoughts. Again he telephoned Ex-Pest.

On this visit, the Ex-Pest men were noticed, or the tenants with cockroaches had told other tenants about their problem, Mr Clark never learned which, and it didn't much matter. One man and two women rang Mr Clark to ask him to ask the exterminator men to come to their apartments.

Mr Clark and the reddish-haired Ex-Pest man had a talk in the service passage at the back of the lobby before the Ex-Pest men departed.

'If you ask me, the cockroaches are all over the building and it's just a question of time – '

'All over it? Don't be silly! This building's hardly six months old! The start of occupancy was less than six months ago.' Naturally, Ex-Pest was trying to drum up a big contract for extensive fumigating, Mr Clark thought.

'All right, sir, you just wait. You'll see.'

'What were you proposing?' asked Mr Clark. 'Or going to propose?'

'Total,' said the Ex-Pest man. 'Total once and for all with our new Ex-Pest Unique. Let's say these cockroaches got here in the building material – '

'New building material?'

'All right, the old stuff was lying around on the ground before this Jade Towers was built, right? Old wood and stuff from the former building. Don't ask me how, but I know roaches! You had a couple hundred men bringing lunch-boxes here, construction guys.' The Ex-Pest man shook his head. 'If you want to go through with it, just give us a call, sir. Otherwise, you're going to have trouble. These fancy people won't put up with cockroaches – like the rest of us in our humble abodes, eh?' With a broad grin, he waved good-bye.

Mr Clark was shocked, debated telling the Jade Towers' Board of Management, and decided not to for the moment. As the Ex-Pest man said, the Jade Towers people were a fancy lot, and maybe exaggerating. Cockroaches simply couldn't be well-established in the Jade Towers, with nests where their eggs had hatched for generations. Sidney Clark associated roaches with old tenement buildings, filthy dumb-waiter shafts down which people dropped garbage in paper bags, buildings with cracks. There were no cracks in the Jade Towers.

'Hey, look at this, Sidney!' said Bernard Newman, a Broadway theatre owner and a tenant of the Jade Towers. He had plopped an afternoon tabloid down on the reception desk top, and was pointing to an item in heavy black type. 'Cockroaches yet!' Bernard Newman grinned.

Sidney Clark read the lines in the 'Town Talk' column, which alternated its paragraphs in normal and dark type. It said:

The much touted and poofed Jade Towers on Lex has just received a custard pie in its face. Certain well-known tenants, who shall be nameless because they want it that way, are bruiting it about in supper-clubs that their expensive digs are plagued with cockroaches – even as yours and mine. One beautifully clad young lady said she was thinking of breaking her lease and clearing out.

Mr Clark shook his head as if he had not heard of roaches in the Jade Towers. 'Have you seen any roaches in your apartment, Mr Newman?'

'No, but a woman asked me that same question yesterday in the elevator. She's seen a couple and was amazed. Lives on a floor way up, she said, maybe a penthouse, I forgot. Crazy, isn't it?' With a friendly smile, Mr Newman picked up his newspaper and strolled off toward the elevators.

At that moment, William C. Fordham, a Wall Street broker, was sitting in the sun in shorts on his penthouse terrace, working from home as usual with computer and telephone on either side of him. He and his girlfriend Phyllis, like most of the tenants in the Jade Towers, hadn't seen a cockroach in their apartment, and hadn't heard a word about cockroaches in the building.

Later that day, when Mr Clark was about to quit his post because the evening desk manager, Paul Vinson, had arrived, a man and woman approached the desk, accompanied by one of the doormen.

'These people are asking about rentals, sir,' said the doorman.

'Good evening,' said Mr Clark. 'For the two of you? . . . One- or two-bedroom?'

'One,' said the woman, 'with a view east if possible. – Is it true that the Jade Towers has a roach problem just now?'

Mr Clark shook his head slowly. 'No, madam. No.'

'That's what we read in the *Post* today. And we heard it from someone yesterday – a friend we told we were going to ask about an apartment here.'

'A new building like this?' Mr Clark smiled. 'I think it's a rumour put out – maybe to be funny.'

'But you've heard about it too,' said the man.

'No. No, I have not,' replied Mr Clark, beginning to think this couple might be journalists snooping. 'Would you like to see our one-bedroom apartments? There're only two left, I believe.'

There was not a cockroach to be seen in either of the one-bedroom apartments that Mr Clark showed Mr and Mrs Ellis, and they took the first one.

Nine days had gone by without a cockroach complaint, when Bertrand Cushings, head of the Board of Management of the Jade Towers, paid a surprise visit. Mr Clark had seen him only twice before, and had received a firm handshake from him, when he had been taken on as one of the three desk managers. Now Mr Cushings was accompanied by a sombre-faced man whose name Mr Clark didn't get. The message Mr Cushings delivered in Mr Clark's office behind the reception desk was that several tenants, more than twenty, in fact, had got together and engaged a lawyer and threatened to break their leases unless something was done about the cockroaches in the Jade Towers.

'You seem to be unaware of all this,' said Mr Cushings.

'Not at all, sir. Ex-Pest was here twice. I sent the Board a report. I haven't had any complaints since.' Mr Clark felt that his face had gone white.

'I don't know what's going on, but I can tell you it's a disgrace,' said Mr Cushings. 'Jokes in the newspapers, letters from lawyers – one from our own lawyer, warning us. You're the one supposed to have his ear to the ground here. You and what's his name – Vinson. And Fred Miller.'

'Yes, sir.' Mr Clark saw in the set of Mr Cushings's jowl that he might have lost his job already, that Mr Cushings had more important things on his mind now – namely millions of dollars – than the verbal sacking of Sidney Clark.

Mr Cushings then began to explain Ex-Pest's plan of attack, but in an absent and murmuring way, as if since Sidney Clark might not be here for the duration of the work, why should he go into detail?

'This'll be a floor by floor attack. Evacuation floor by floor, all expenses paid by the Jade Towers, until this roach problem is licked. But you'll have all this on paper. The desk managers will,' Mr Cushings added, as if the desk managers might be other people soon.

Mr Cushings and his colleague departed.

As if to underline Cushings's words, a telephone call came then for Sidney Clark: a woman in 49 L had seen at least six cockroaches darting away two minutes ago, when she had come home and turned on the light in her kitchen.

'Not the first time,' she said, 'but six at once! I thought I really must report this . . .'

Sidney Clark said reassuringly that the entire building was going to be fumigated, and that the problem was in good hands.

When Paul Vinson came behind the desk, Mr Clark told him about Cushings's visit.

'Floor by floor evacuation,' Vinson said. 'That's going to cost the Jade Towers a pretty penny.'

Sidney Clark, at around 10 the next morning, received by messenger the Ex-Pest Disinfectant Plan, and signed for it. The envelope was addressed to him and Mr Vinson and Mr Miller. It contained a detailed schedule of the floor by floor disinfecting with Ex-Pest Unique, which would begin with basement and ground floors, necessitating closure of the Jade Cup and the Jade Corner piano bar, and of course everything else on the ground floor, the florist's and so on, for 'not more than forty-eight hours'. At the same time, the tenants of the second floor (the one above ground floor) would quit their apartments for forty-eight hours, and the procedure would be repeated in subsequent days. The desk services such as reception, presence of managers and doormen, would continue as usual. Tenants would be notified individually of their dates for evacuation. An acceleration in disinfecting was anticipated after ten days, so that three floors at a time would be evacuated during a forty-eight-hour period, resulting in the operation being completed in about one month.

The news of this directive was leaked somehow and reported in a couple of newspapers the next day.

'Some of our residents are justifiably annoyed by the presence of any kind of vermin in our building,' said Cushings to the press, and this appeared in the *Times*. 'A small fault becomes a big one here, and that's the way the Jade Towers prefers its residents to react. That's why we're going to solve the current problem as quickly and efficiently as is humanly possible.'

'Roach parties' started in the Jade Towers, as the extermination programme gathered momentum. In apartments and at the swimming pool, people were supposed to look out for cockroaches and count how many they had seen. A high-score man or woman was presumed to have won. A wag had floated some large jade-coloured roaches made of painted balloons in the swimming pool. This somehow got photographed, and appeared in *New York* magazine.

The better hotels were said to be enjoying extra patronage, with Jade Towers tenants being put up for at least two days and in fine style. Then there were tall stories about super-cockroaches which, having fed on caviar and buttery croissants, had grown to great size and boldness, fending off workmen who wanted to enter apartments to fumigate. Another story told of cockroaches which had captured an elevator and were using it to go up and down as they pleased, taking themselves to safer floors, and frightening off, by their number, workmen who tried to smoke them out.

This last story might have been closest to the truth. Some cockroaches may have used the elevators, if only by accident, but all the insects still alive were going upward. Ex-Pest had anticipated this, which was why the enemy was being attacked from the ground floor upward. Cockroaches became more in evidence on the upper floors by the time Ex-Pest reached the fortieth floor. The courteous letters to the Jade Towers tenants from the Board of Management now asked for a four-floor evacuation per day '. . . to hasten the work and minimise inconvenience . . .'

Many tenants on the upper floors smiled cynically at this. They were already inconvenienced good and plenty by darting cock-roaches, but two things influenced them in the direction of hanging on: the substitute housing in good hotels offered by the Jade Towers, and the fact that the majority of residents wanted to keep their apartments because of safety and comfort (apart from the current cockroach situation) and its accruing prestige, even. Years from now, some said, people would ask, 'Were you really in the Jade Towers during the great cockroach cleanup?'

Ex-Pest sweepers and vacuum cleaner pushers had meanwhile tidied up the lower floors, while Jade Towers guards watched, as they had during fumigation, to be sure there was no pilfering and that clothing or whatever was not damaged. The apartments were then aired.

Tenants of the higher storeys told Mr Clark and Mr Vinson of seeing 'a few amazingly large cockroaches' in their kitchens and bathrooms, and of using their own sprays in the interim before their date for evacuation came round. Sidney Clark and Paul Vinson were still on duty, as was Fred Miller, putting on brave faces, and beginning to think they might not lose their jobs after all, if they weathered, like captains in a storm, this roach season, which surely had a limit, just seven days from now on a Wednesday. Meanwhile, the three had their hands full with telephoning for hotel rooms ahead of schedule, because many upper-floor tenants suddenly wanted to get out all at once. Big cockroaches had been seen on the slopes in the centre of the swimming pool, for instance, and no one wanted to use the pool any longer.

An elegant old lady who lived on the eighty-sixth floor under the swimming pool, and was the matriarch of one of the wealthiest families in America, laid a thick envelope on the reception desk one afternoon when Sidney Clark was on duty. 'It isn't funny any more, despite all the jokes,' the old lady said sourly. 'This is a carbon copy. The original will be sent registered post to the Board of Management.' With a rap of her cane, she turned toward the door and toddled off, accompanied by her female secretary and her man servant, both of whom lived in the apartment with her.

Mr Clark opened the envelope with slightly trembling fingers. Mrs Mildred Pringle of 86 H stated that after ridding her kitchen of cockroaches at some trouble and inconvenience to herself and household, she had discovered that 'huge roaches' had attacked the clothing in her closets, including three fur coats, for which a bill would be sent after she had consulted with her insurance company. She gave notice that she intended to break her lease and quit her apartment within two days, or as soon as removal service could be arranged.

The lobby at that moment was a-bustle, as it had been ever since the Ex-Pest assault, with tenants and liveried errand boys carrying suitcases in and out, and doormen going back and forth to inform people that their taxi was waiting outside. The switchboard girls, three, were occupied mainly with tenants wanting to know if their hotel rooms had been confirmed so that they could leave.

Sidney Clark had had a couple of bad dreams about cockroaches, about turning on the light in his own small and immaculate kitchen, and seeing the walls all a-quiver with alarmed cockroaches clambering over one another as they fled. And Paul Vinson had told him – as if reality followed Sidney's dream – a story of his having been summoned at 3 a.m. by an angry man in an apartment in the fifties floors (which were presumably now free of roaches), the man had turned the light on in his kitchen, and Vinson had seen at least a hundred flitting behind the breadbox, up under the cupboards, into corners anywhere. Now as Sidney Clark looked at the activity in the big lobby, the scowls of some people, the what-the-hell grins of others, his dreams seemed more and more like reality. Was Ex-Pest winning?

Sidney Clark was now working several hours per day overtime, and so was Vinson, neither intending to ask for overtime pay, but preferring to hold on to their jobs, if they could. Both thought (and so did Fred Miller) that the Board of Management was using them, letting them take the flak during the roach crisis, and that Cushings intended to sack them once the extermination programme was finished. The Ex-Pest men, though there were three shifts, also worked overtime, came and went through the service entrance of the Jade Towers at all hours of the day and night, and something like thirty of them in dark green uniforms must have been working at any time round the clock.

And still complaints came in at the desk. One man had returned to his apartment on the fifty-seventh floor to find 'irreparable damage' to many of his books and papers, despite his having covered them with plastic sheets which he had taped to the floor. He intended 'to seek recompense' from the Jade Towers' Board of Management. A woman tenant had found that cockroaches had got into three of her oriental rugs, which had been rolled up and sealed in heavy brown paper, and had damaged them 'beyond repair, at least in this country', and she was going to take legal action.

The reddish-haired Ex-Pest man turned up that same day at the reception desk. Now Mr Clark did not consider his appearance in the lobby so inappropriate, and some people standing about with luggage greeted him as if they knew him. The Ex-Pest man was pink in the face and sweaty from his exertions.

'Fresh air smells good down here,' he remarked to Sidney Clark. 'Have you got a glass of water back there? I'm still thirsty.' He indicated the open door of the office behind the desk, came round the desk and accepted the glass of water that Mr Clark handed him. 'Wow! *Upstairs!* – Those cockroaches are laying eggs faster than normal, I swear!' He wiped his lips with his bare forearm.

'Wh-what floor are you on today?'

'Eighty-fifth and -sixth. We're on schedule and gettin' there, but *man*! No tenants up on top now, y'know, just us and the roaches. Ha-ha!'

Mr Clark knew that the penthouses had been evacuated for nearly a week, the swimming pool kept half full, but the water poisoned, because many roaches came there to drink. As if on cue with Sidney Clark's thoughts, the Ex-Pest man said:

'We keep an eye on the pool, maybe a couple thousand dead floating in it every day and we suck 'em off, but we've seen these extra large cockroaches walking down the side and drinking and going away again. Y'been up there?'

'No,' said Mr Clark. Was this a dream? But he could see the Ex-Pest man's sturdy thigh on the edge of a desk, where Mr Clark wished he hadn't parked himself. 'But you're bound to be achieving something. You say you're removing a lot of dead roaches too.' Mr Clark moved toward the office door, to indicate that he had to get back to the desk.

'Sure, but the ones way up there are mostly bigger, and they're not dying so fast, that's what's interesting. And they're multiplying faster. Rats do that too, y'know, after an extermination programme, to fill in the gaps in their population. Did you know that? – Well, I'll split. Thanks for the water.'

A couple of people were waiting at the reception desk, and one of the switchboard girls was trying to cope. Mr Clark squared his shoulders and advanced.

'Hey!' called the Ex-Pest man. 'If you come up, ask for Ricky!' He jabbed his chest with his thumb. 'You won't recognise me in my gear up there.'

Sidney Clark thought that it might make a good impression on the Board if he could say that he had paid a visit upstairs to see how the work was progressing. So when Paul Vinson arrived in early afternoon, Mr Clark left the desk. He rode up in an elevator with a silent man and woman who got off in the fifties, kept on going up with a definite feeling that he was about to enter a danger zone, something like a battlefield where bullets might be flying. Absurd, he told himself. Some thirty men were working where he was going, and no deaths or even injuries had been reported as yet.

'Here, got a suit for you,' said a figure Mr Clark could not recognise, but he knew the voice as Ricky's.

Ricky wore a head-to-toe dark green overall with a plastic

rectangle where his eyes were, so he could see out. 'Zip up the front. You don't have to worry about the air – for a while.'

The air smelt lemony, not like a healthy citrus scent, but rather synthetic. Apartment doors stood open, and green-swathed figures came and went in the corridor whose jade floor was covered with electric lines, tubes, spray tanks on wheels, vacuum machines whose tubes led to a central container three times the size of a metal garbage can. The shouts of the men to one another were muffled and unintelligible.

'Show you what we're *up* against!' yelled Ricky close to Sidney Clark's ear. 'This way!'

Ricky opened an apartment door, which had been unlocked, and they entered a noisier atmosphere, where four or five men fired sprayers from Ex-Pest Unique tanks strapped to their backs. They aimed the stuff behind bookcases that were covered with plastic sheets, under sofas and couches. Mr Clark was sweating already. He looked down at the floor and jumped a little. Cockroaches were twitching, rolling over one another – one turned on its back and remained so – others dashed directionlessly, and they were of all sizes, from what Mr Clark considered normal size to nearly three inches long. He stamped a foot to shake off a few that had crawled on to his green-covered lower leg.

'All these'll die!' Ricky shouted. 'Don't worry, they can't get into your suit! They've come up from the lower floors!'

Sidney Clark kicked at a large cockroach which seemed determined to attach itself to him. Christ! He peered up through the rectangular plastic before his eyes, and saw that the high white ceiling glistened with the shiny, light-brown backs of cockroaches, all trembling, some dropping as he watched.

Ricky patted his shoulder reassuringly. 'Tomorrow the vacuum boys'll be in for the corpses! Let's go!'

They next visited a vacuum-stage apartment, where it was impossible to talk because of the din. To Sidney Clark's disgust, he saw live cockroaches being sucked up from the floor, along with crusty, motionless hundreds. Had all the cockroaches in New York come here?

'... *burnt!*' Ricky roared in Mr Clark's ear. 'Below!' Ricky pointed downward, maybe to indicate basement furnaces.

When they were out in the corridor again, Ricky shouted, 'Want to see the swimming pool?'

Mr Clark shook his head, gave a polite smile that Ricky could not see and, gesturing downward, said that he had to get back to work. As he glanced at the nearby elevator doors, Mr Clark noticed two fat cockroaches squeezing themselves with difficulty, but making it, into the crack between the floor and the elevator shaft doors. They were not committing suicide down the shaft, he knew, but would climb upward, away from the ascending fumes. Sidney Clark got out of his suit, and entered the elevator that Ricky had summoned and was holding.

'You give us a good report!' yelled Ricky. 'Because we're winding this up Wednesday, coupla days ahead of schedule!'

That night, Sidney Clark had no bad dreams, because he couldn't sleep. When he closed his eyes, he saw twitching roaches, long antennae trembling, seeking a way to flee. Their backs glistened as if with oil, they covered every surface in Sidney Clark's imagination – walls, ceilings, floors. Nonsense, he told himself. He gave a tremendous sigh, because he had been holding his breath. He'd seen the vacuums taking up hundreds in seconds, dead for ever. The cockroaches *were* going upward to inevitable destruction, and tenants of the Jade Towers were moving back. The second to sixtieth floors had nearly all their tenants back, except those who happened to be travelling, and nearly a hundred tenants were due back in the next two days. Floors up to the seventy-fifth had been declared 'disinfected and fume-free', but the Board was giving tenants an extra day in their hotels, if they so wished, as a gesture of goodwill and also to try to avoid complaints about headache among tenants who might be sensitive to Ex-Pest Unique's fumes.

But against this Sidney Clark had to weigh, in all honesty, the fact that at least three tenants, even apart from the rich Mrs Pringle, had moved their furniture and their belongings from their apartments today, rather yesterday, as it was now 4 a.m. And there had been Bernard Newman again just before noon, with another newspaper item to show him, something about *Supercockroach* in heavy type over a paragraph that said that Lexington Avenue's Jade Towers, which had for half a year topped all in the Big Apple for luxurious apartment living, had now topped all in the size of its cockroaches, and that the current cleanup was driving the huge varmints upward to the penthouses.

Mr Clark, bleary-eyed but spruce as ever in a dark business suit and white shirt with french cuffs, was at the reception desk by 9 a.m.

He put on a smile of welcome for returning tenants. Ricky telephoned down, sounding tired but cheerful as he said: 'We're winding up the penthouses today, and that's the end, except for the towers, and we might have a question about them.'

'The towers? But nobody lives in the towers!' The towers were simply hollow domes with some metal bars inside to support them. Mr Clark had been up to see the towers once.

'Still, we want to do a thorough job, sir. – Want to come up and see the pool? No water in it now, but it's clean as a whistle, all shiny jade tiles again.'

Mr Clark said he was glad to hear that, but he was too busy at the desk to come up.

Around 3 that afternoon, Ricky telephoned again, and asked if Mr Clark and Mr Vinson could come up, because he had 'an urgent question'. Ricky sounded so urgent that Mr Clark agreed to come up. Mr Clark interrupted Paul Vinson to tell him the situation, and asked Madeleine, one of the switchboard girls, to hold the desk for a few minutes.

The two went up, and Ricky met them with green zip suits. 'Just for safety!' yelled Ricky. They were at penthouse level, and again Sidney Clark looked on to a scene of tubes, cables and rolling vacuum tanks. He saw some roaches on the floor, too, but to his relief these seemed all dead.

'The problem's *up*!' said Ricky, beckoning.

They entered a service section with a staircase up and down, one of the fire escape stairways, and here it seemed Ex-Pest had not yet started work. Mr Clark saw hundreds of rather large roaches crawling nervously about on the metal staircase, as if changing their minds over and over again in a split-second about whether to go up or down, but most were definitely climbing the stairs.

'Only the biggest are still making it after all the fumes,' said Ricky. 'Now here's the problem – '

They were now on the level roof, under the sky. There were many roaches crawling around on the grey surface of the roof, walking in all directions, but somewhat aimlessly, and it occurred to Sidney Clark that they would have to jump to their deaths to escape, but on the other hand, how could fumes kill them in the open air? And couldn't they simply walk down the sides of the building? And should all these cockroaches have been allowed to get up here in the first place? He was about to ask a question, when Ricky said:

'They're all up here, see?' Ricky indicated not the tower nearer them but the other tower some fifteen yards away, where five or six green-clad workers, some on ladders, pointed hose nozzles upward into the dome. 'We can't get 'em all this way and we want to *torch* 'em!'

Sidney Clark was alarmed at the thought of fire. He certainly couldn't give permission on his own. He turned to Paul Vinson, who was nervously tapping Sidney Clark's arm, and saying something he couldn't hear.

'Sprayers can't finish 'em off!' Ricky yelled at both men. 'Air's not confined up there and the domes're full of 'em! Look!' From a pocket in his suit, Ricky pulled a big flashlight and held it in his gloved hand, directing it up at the dome's interior.

Sidney Clark took a step back in horror. He had seen a quivering circle, maybe twenty feet in diameter, of madly active cockroaches, clinging to one another, not able to go any higher, and not able to escape.

'Y'see my *point*!' yelled Ricky. 'Torchin' 'em's the only way!'

Paul Vinson gave a muffled cry, and swayed as if about to faint.

Laughing, Ricky grabbed Vinson's arm, and unzipped his head covering, so that Vinson could get some air. 'Go down, go ahead down!' Ricky pointed to the open doorway which led to the stairs.

'I really must ask the Board about using *fire*!' said Mr Clark, also drifting toward the open doorway, and promising to be in touch as soon as he knew what the Board decided.

Mr Clark and Mr Vinson shed their protective suits, and rode down in an express elevator.

'Look at that!' cried Paul Vinson, pointing to a cockroach which appeared to be six inches long in a front corner of the elevator floor.

It was laying an egg! Both men retreated to the opposite corner of the elevator, though the cockroach seemed to be paying them no mind, certainly wasn't facing them. The egg emerged in a brown rectangular form, nearly as large as the little cakes of soap that the Jade Towers dispensed in cardboard boxes on the rims of bathroom basins, if tenants used the housekeeping staff for their apartment cleaning. *Step on the roach and the egg*, Sidney Clark told himself, but he couldn't. He hadn't the guts.

'Christ,' he said wearily to Paul Vinson. The elevator arrived at ground floor, they both stepped out, and Sidney Clark at once pushed the button for penthouse, and sent the parturient cockroach up.

Mr Clark telephoned the Board, could not reach Cushings, but spoke to a man who sounded appalled at the idea of torching the interior of the towers, though Mr Clark told him that there appeared to be nothing inflammable in them, just some metal supports. The man said he would be over right away, and hung up.

Paul Vinson had gone home, sick or claiming to be, so Sidney Clark was busy. Lots of tenants were coming back today, inquiring about mail and messages.

'I see you're celebrating today,' said a young woman whom Mr Clark recognised, Susan Dulcey, an actress who lived on one of the higher floors. 'Fireworks on the roof. Very pretty. Have you seen them?'

Mr Clark shook his head and smiled. 'No, I haven't. Not yet. Welcome back, Miss Dulcey!' Fireworks? Mr Clark took the first opportunity to go outside and have a look. It was around 6 p.m., and dusk was falling.

People were standing on the sidewalk across the street, gawking up, pointing, laughing. From among them, even across busy Lexington Avenue, Sidney Clark thought he heard the word '... *roaches* ...' Or was he becoming obsessed? He crossed the avenue on a red light. He could see reddish-orange sparks shooting and drifting from the lower edges of the twin domes – each spark a cockroach; he knew – and he could hear, or did he imagine hearing, the crackle of cockroaches sizzling into oblivion? The towers themselves glowed an orangey-pink, as if they might be about to melt from the torches' heat, and more frightening was the rim of pink that marked the top edge of the building. Or could that be a reflection of the towers' fires?

'Anyone for fried roaches?' a male voice in the crowd asked.

'Ha-ha! Nah, it's some kind of fireworks!'

'No!' said another voice. 'I can see workmen up there! They've got blow-torches!' The man speaking was holding binoculars to his eyes.

'Can I have a quick look through those?' asked a woman.

Sidney Clark trotted back to his desk. What next, a fire, he wondered? Would the next horrid sound be that of a fire engine making its screaming way through Lexington Avenue traffic?

'Hello, Mr Clark,' said an incoming tenant. 'Any letters for

Simpson, fifty-nine H? – Thanks! The fireworks look nice on the roof. Today's sort of special, eh?'

Mr Clark returned Mr Simpson's smile. 'It certainly is. We've got a clean house now.'

'Mr Clark – telephone for you,' said a switchboard girl.

'Kellerman in seven J,' a man's voice said. 'I've seen *four* roaches in the last ten minutes since I got home from work and they're all Bermuda-sized! If you don't believe me, come up! I heard those exterminator guys're still here, so send *them* up too, would you?'

'I *am* sorry, Mr Kellerman. I'll be up myself right away. Thank you for phoning.' Mr Clark told a girl to buzz Ex-Pest on the penthouse floor and send someone to 7 J at once. Then he hurried to an elevator.

If there were any cockroaches in this elevator, Mr Clark did not know, because he didn't look, and it was a short ride to the seventh floor, where he found the corridor rather busy.

Kellerman's door stood open, so did at least three other apartment doors, and a couple of women were talking excitedly together in the corridor.

'Oh, Mr Clark!' one woman said. 'Those roaches aren't gone! There're two in my kitchen and I can't even scare them off the drainboard!'

'My bathroom,' said the other woman with a pained face. 'Would you come in and look?'

Mr Clark gestured toward Kellerman's apartment. 'As soon as I answer this call, Mrs – ' He went quickly into 7 J.

'This way,' said Kellerman, a large man in shirtsleeves, motioning toward his bathroom.

A monstrous cockroach, truly five inches long, floated in Kellerman's bathtub, which held several inches of water.

'Good heavens!' said Mr Clark. The cockroach floated facing Mr Clark, motionless but not dead, he saw, because the long flexible antennae moved lazily from left to right. Some of its three pairs of legs stirred, the cockroach turned a little, and Mr Clark was reminded bizarrely of a fat person lolling on the surface of a swimming pool.

'How about *that*?' Mr Kellerman asked. 'I was getting ready to take a bath. So much for these Ex-Pest jerks!' He picked up a toilet brush and whammed the cockroach with the back of it.

Water splashed, and Mr Clark stepped back.

The blow roused the brown insect to activity, it swam to the tub's back end, and climbed with giant strides up the slanting enamel to the tub's rim and stopped, facing them.

'Okay, you kill it,' said Mr Kellerman. 'I swear I've had it and I'm not staying another night here.'

'I have to say the same.' This was from one of the two women from the corridor, who had come into Kellerman's apartment and was standing just outside the bathroom door. 'Excuse me for intruding. My husband just came home, Mr Clark, and we're going to . . .'

Sidney Clark nodded nervously, and made his way to the apartment door. There were more voices and people in the corridor, and some tried to get his attention.

'Is this a joke?' one young man asked, looking ready to hit Mr Clark with his fist.

Sidney Clark thought the elevator would never come. 'I'm going to speak to Ex-Pest – to the Board – '

'The nerve of them!' cried a woman. 'Getting us out and then back to *this*!'

Mr Clark darted into the elevator and jabbed the button for ground floor, then realised that a man and woman with suitcases were also in the elevator, and a second later noticed two rectangular objects, which he now knew were cockroach egg sacs, on the elevator floor.

'Mr Clark, what *is* going on?' asked the woman. 'Absolutely huge roaches all over the building! My husband and I are going to stay with friends tonight.'

'And nice of them to take us in,' her husband added. He was elderly, as was his wife. 'They'll want to fumigate *us*, I'd imagine.'

Mr Clark couldn't recollect their name. 'We're speaking with the exterminating people now, sir.'

Ground floor. Mr Clark remembered his manners, helped the woman with her suitcase, and let the two precede him. The lobby was chock-a-block with people, suitcases, even a few trunks, and everyone seemed to be talking at once.

'. . . *finished*!' said an angry female voice.

'No way! Ha-ha-ha! . . . Want to share a taxi?'

'. . . like the ones in *my* apartment! My Dobermann's afraid of them!'

Mr Clark made his way to the reception desk, where he found Ricky with his back against the desk, besieged by questioners.

'. . . everything under control, I swear,' Ricky was saying. 'Naturally just a few – very few of the biggest survived.' Ricky was hooted down, and he wiped his sweating forehead with his arm. He had pushed back his head covering, and he looked like an outer-space traveller in green instead of white.

It did not escape Sidney Clark that the people in the lobby were laughing at Ricky's efficient-looking uniform and at his efforts to explain the presence of giant cockroaches as a 'normal development'.

'The weaker strains *have* been exterminated – by us,' Ricky was saying to people around him. 'All we need is a different agent to kill what's here now.'

Ricky was clinging to his job, Mr Clark realised, doing his best to save the Jade Towers too.

'These cockroaches belong in the *zoo*!' yelled a man. 'Behind bars!'

A lot of people laughed.

'I think this place is on *fire*!' This from a woman who had just rushed into the lobby. 'The roof! Go out and look!'

'Now we've had it!' said a man.

Sidney Clark heard the dreaded moan of a fire engine's siren, close, he realised, or he wouldn't have heard it through the din in the lobby. '*Ricky!*' he yelled. 'What's happening on the roof?'

'Nothing!' Ricky replied, with a tired wave of his hand. 'We got water up there. Sure, we're torchin' 'em as they come.'

'What do you mean "as they come"?' asked a man.

'They're climbin' up, sure. Layin' faster than normal, and we've gotta torch the egg cases too, natch.' Ricky rested an elbow on the reception desk top in an attitude of self-assurance, but his words provoked jeers from the listeners.

People were departing via the glass doors, and others, struggling with luggage and coats over their arms, poured out of the elevators. Strangers, Sidney Clark saw to his alarm, were coming in from the street. Strangers meant theft to Sidney Clark.

'Michael!' Mr Clark called sharply to a doorman. 'Who're these boys coming in?'

'They say they've got appointments. They give names,' Michael replied.

'Keep them out!' said Mr Clark. 'Repeat *out*!'

The switchboard girls were overbusy as were the doormen, trying to cope with calls for taxis, maybe complaints too. But no, the complaint stage was past, Mr Clark realised. He was witnessing a mass exodus.

'Madeleine!' Sidney Clark called. 'Have you tried to reach Cushings?'

'Yes, sir, two hours ago. Mr Cushings won't come.'

It was like the captain abandoning his ship. Was he supposed to be the captain now? 'Did Paul come back?'

'No, sir,' said Madeleine hastily, and turned back to her buzzing board.

A bell clanged outside, and Mr Clark saw a fire engine at the kerb. Was the place really on fire?

'Oh! – Watch out!' With these words, a woman instantly cleared a space around her. 'Eeek! – My *God*!'

'Step on it, my brave fellows! Ha-ha-ha!'

Mr Clark knew that it must be a huge roach which was walking toward the door, judging from the swath in the downward-looking crowd. The doormen looked down too, and not one of the four big men made an effort to kill it.

Two firemen who hurried in, heading for the elevators, raised a cynical cheer from the changing and mostly merry people in the lobby. Television people were here! One came in on a rolling ladder, filming from a height.

'Here's one! Get this one!' A woman pointed to a wall near her.

Mr Clark realised that the strangers he had seen barging in were the TV crew – or some of them were – because now they were hitching up their lights to the electric outlets in the lobby, and without so much as a by your leave. He made a dash for the door, curious about the fire situation on the roof. He found the sidewalk crowded, cops and firemen urging the crowd back from the door-way.

'Is there a fire?' Mr Clark asked a cop.

'No, false alarm,' the cop replied. 'Smoke up there and someone turned on an alarm. *Roach* smoke!' The cop was smiling.

People stared at the fire engine, stared up and pointed. The sidewalk bore great black crumbs of cockroach carcasses, and some people looked up warily and dusted their shoulders, yet lingered, fascinated.

'Disgusting!' said a woman, moving on.

'Look!' a small boy cried, pointing. *'Jeepers!'*

A big cockroach was crossing the sidewalk toward the street, rather slowly, and Mr Clark saw that it was in the process of laying an egg, and consequently looked nearly twice as long as any he had seen so far. Women shrieked. Men said things like, 'Amazing! – But it's really a cockroach, I can see that!'

The fire engine pulled away, and taxis at once took its place at the kerb. TV cameras ground, filming the notables and the not so notable who were trickling out of the Jade Towers with their luggage.

'Do you intend to sue, Miss Dulcey?' a man asked.

'Don't know yet,' replied Miss Dulcey with a smile, following Michael who was carrying her suitcases to a cab.

It seemed that no one was staying in the Jade Towers overnight. It was past 9 p.m., Sidney Clark saw to his surprise. The TV crews were gathering their long cables. Some of the Ex-Pest men, looking exhausted, straggled into the lobby in quest of Ricky.

Ricky was standing near the reception desk, talking to a TV man. 'We're going to clear it up. Maybe not tonight . . .'

Another shift of switchboard girls had come on, and all three were talking. People were inquiring about the safety of their furniture and possessions, Mr Clark gathered.

'Our doormen will be on duty as usual,' one girl said to someone.

'Paul, go get us something to eat, would you?' Ricky said to one of his men. 'I can't leave.'

'There's the Jade Cup,' said Mr Clark. 'Eggs and hamburgers – '

'Jade Cup's been closed since this morning,' an Ex-Pest man interrupted. 'You should've seen the roaches in there! The big ones came down, y'see, and made for that kitchen. The lady manager – Well, the waitresses all quit this morning.'

'Just because the roaches became immune to Ex-Pest Unique,' Ricky said to Sidney Clark. 'Now when we – '

'I'm *sick* of it! You've failed in your work and you've cost me my job!' Mr Clark said, because the TV man had departed.

'Want to see what we're up against?' Ricky said. 'Show him, Joey! Any corridor. Try the second.'

Joey and, reluctantly, Sidney Clark, climbed the service stairs to the second floor. Mr Clark saw roaches going up and down these stairs, maybe thirty of them, of all sizes. Ricky came with them, and he still had the energy to stamp on a few, cursing as he did so, but he was choosing the smaller, or younger insects, Mr Clark noticed.

Ricky pulled aside a stone cigarette ash receptacle, which stood beside the elevators. 'See this?' One egg sac and two cockroaches were revealed, in what Mr Clark took to be a mating position. 'And it's the goddam egg bags everywhere, *hidden* under everything. Under the carpets – Who's going to find all these – ever?' asked Ricky rhetorically. 'In closet corners, in some little crack in a bookcase – It's hopeless.'

'Then what's to be done?' asked Sidney Clark, who still had a feeling that something could be done, even if it took time. 'Develop a new insecticide?'

'By the time we develop it – this place – ' He waved a hand. 'Torch it, that's my advice.'

The building? Sidney Clark was horrified. 'I'm going out to get something to eat. I missed lunch and I'm bushed.'

They all went down, and found that Paul and another man had returned with containers of coffee and bags full of sandwiches. Mr Clark was invited to join them, and they ate at low tables in the lobby, of which there were quite enough for the thirty-odd men.

Ricky looked better after a couple of sandwiches and a container of coffee, but he was still saying quietly to Sidney Clark, 'Torch it, you'll see. It's a loss, okay, but there's insurance, isn't there? This is an Act of God thing, no? These cockroaches?'

The words haunted Sidney Clark that night as he fitfully slept. *Act of God.* Cockroaches! Cushings's silence was ominous. Was he planning to torch the Jade Towers? When would he himself get notice that he was jobless?

A weary Sidney Clark was on duty at 9 the next morning, and the Jade Towers was again busy, with removal men now, and instead of taxis at the kerb, there was a row of vans. Muscular shirtsleeved men stood around the lobby, waiting their turn to pull up their vans at one of the two larger doors in front and in back. The disorder that they presented illustrated the collapse of everything, it seemed to Sidney Clark. The three switchboard girls looked as if they hadn't slept much either, and there was something desperate in the courtesy with which they spoke to every caller. A couple of newspapers on the reception desk, the *Times* and the *Daily News*, had pictures of a cockroach said to be five and three-quarter inches long, which had been photographed at the Jade Towers.

Dollies with crates and cardboard boxes of household goods, with chairs and upended sofas, standing lamps, tables and desks and carpets, rolled all day toward the front or the back doors, and men shouted to one another, directing the pushers to wait or come ahead. They were going to work all night, one man told Sidney Clark, because the tenants were in a hurry to get their things out and into storage.

By noon, the switchboard girl Madeleine was in tears. 'Mr Clark, they're all sueing! We had at least fifteen calls this morning – and some people wanted to speak to you. We didn't pass them on to you. We said – said the desk officer was somewhere else at the moment.'

Sidney Clark was touched. 'That's kind of you, Madeleine. Go and get some lunch somewhere.'

There followed a week of further disgrace for the Jade Towers, of jokes in the newspapers, and comments from people who had been tenants, some grim, others the 'I surrender graciously to the super-roach' kind of thing.

The Jade Towers was not put to the torch by hired torchers, as many predicted. Lawsuits from apartment owners and lease-holders bankrupted the Jade Towers owners, in spite of the Board of Management's winning its suit against Ex-Pest, which had bankrupted Ex-Pest. Many were the damage claims for cockroach-chewed carpets, upholstery and books, and to lesser extent clothing.

Only days after Ex-Pest had quit the scene, tacitly acknowledging the victory of the larger cockroaches, the Jade Towers stood empty, save for shifts of armed guards on duty day and night inside the front and back doors. New Yorkers and out-of-towners still gazed up at the tall building, but with a different kind of wonder now: it was a ghost building, inhabited by such large insects that people were afraid to live there.

Ideas still came: seal the whole building and smoke the insects to death. Make the Jade Towers start repaying for itself by opening a 'Cellophane Bar' on the ground floor. An architect's plan was drawn up for this, the cellophane walls of the bar-with-piano would be taped to the floor and ceiling, ventilation assured by in and out fans, no food would be served, lest it attract roaches. But this never got off the ground, because there was too much negativity in the air: some cockroaches would still be walking around on the ground floor, wouldn't they? Patrons of the Cellophane Bar would soon stop thinking this was amusing.

Sidney Clark lost his job, along with the rest of the personnel, and received not a bad reference letter from the Board, though it was not a very good one. So he still had hopes of another, similar job. All New York knew of the travail that the Jade Towers staff had gone through in its efforts to conquer the cockroaches.

The building was for sale, of course, though there was no for sale sign on it. The newspapers said 'it has been rumoured' (though it was true) that a couple of exterminating companies had come to take a look at the cockroach problem in the Jade Towers and had declined to take on the job. What were the cockroaches eating? The wall-to-wall carpeting in several apartments? The water had been cut off. But some remained in the pipes, and it rained, and the roaches had access to the roof. They lived. Some people claimed to have seen large roaches leaving the Jade Towers by night, presumably in quest of another building where there might be food. But this was never proved.

The Jade Towers' security guards had demanded and got 'nuisance pay' for working in proximity to the insects, which they swore were growing ever larger. The guards were bored, of course, during their eight-hour shifts, since people kept their distance from the Jade Towers, and no one had tried to enter by stealth or force. The guards devised a game in the long service hall on the ground floor. They baited the back of the hall with sandwich crumbs, and shot at the cockroaches 'from a fair distance' with air-rifles.

'In the long run, we may kill more than the exterminators ever did,' one guard told an inquiring reporter.

The guard added that in twenty-four hours, he and his co-workers shot maybe a thousand, and they swept up the corpses and disposed of them in garbage bins which were emptied as ever at the back of the Jade Towers by the city garbage service.

Incredible, Sidney Clark thought, the Jade Towers having become a shooting gallery whose targets were cockroaches. Or maybe this shooting was another of the wild stories of which the newspapers seemed so fond? One day, when an appointment for a possible job took him past the Jade Towers, Sidney went to the back of the building and put his ear close to the grey metal doors that closed off the service corridor from the street. He heard it: a muffled, even gentle *pop – pop-pop* followed by laughter.

It was true.

Maybe a thousand shot dead each day. Sidney didn't want to

think about it. The cockroaches had become some incomprehensible statistic, like the national debt, or the population of the earth by the year 2000. Okay, let them shoot, he thought. They weren't going to diminish the cockroach population of the Jade Towers by any discernible measure.

RENT-A-WOMB VS. THE
MIGHTY RIGHT

Alicia Newton had never given much thought to the subject of surrogate mothers, until the Sunday her parents told her that the Reverend Townsend had based his sermon on it. This was at their Sunday midday meal, after her parents had come home from church.

'He even mentioned Frick Medical Center,' said Alicia's mother. 'Didn't you tell me that Geoff had done a few of these operations, Alicia?'

Dr Geoffrey Robinson, Alicia's fiancé, was an obstetrician at Frick Medical Center.

'I'm sure Geoff's done some,' Alicia replied. 'But his main work is deliveries and some pre-natal – '

'Townsend was saying the surrogate mother business is becoming a racket. To make money,' said her father, carving more pork roast.

Alicia supposed that Townsend had quoted something from the Old Testament about the wrongness of interfering with nature. 'It's not particularly profitable for Frick, as far as I know. It's such a short procedure, taking the egg out under a local.'

'Profitable for the *surrogate mothers*,' Alicia's mother said. 'How're they recruited, dear?'

Alicia paused, puzzled. 'They're not recruited, Mommie, they volunteer. Lots of young women need the money, true, but it's just a normal fee plus some maintenance, I think.'

'Normal fee? Ten thousand dollars and up?' said her father.

'I don't think there's a fixed rate. It's by private contract,' said Alicia. 'But the point is, a surrogate mother is for couples who can't have a baby. If the wife is infertile or keeps miscarrying, for instance.'

After a few murmurings from her parents, the subject was dropped, but the atmosphere remained a bit stiff, Alicia felt. Her parents had always been conservative, and in the last couple of years more so, in Alicia's opinion, maybe because of the new conservatism in Meadsville's churches (the town had more churches than schools), and what the Mighty Right was putting out via TV and radio. The Mighty Right was headed by the Reverend Jimmy Birdshall, and had its own TV and radio stations and publishing houses that printed fundamentalist magazines. The TV and radio stations asked for donations from the public and got them, so Birdshall had the money to support right-wing candidates running for all kinds of offices, from representatives in Congress to Attorney General. This bolstered the conservative President and had already led to conservatives being appointed to the Supreme Court. Birdshall – called Birdshit by his opponents – could shout his fundamentalism everywhere in America, because of his money.

Alicia's father David Newton was in the real estate business and had to keep on the good side of everybody, so he and her mother now went to church every Sunday, as did nearly everybody else in town. Her mother was active in local welfare societies and women's clubs dedicated to good causes. Alicia had been encouraged to 'do something for the public good', so she had taken up nursing in the middle of university years, finished an arduous course, and now at twenty-two was employed at Frick Medical Center on the edge of town. There she had met Geoff whom she adored, and they intended to marry in a few months. At least her parents approved of Geoff, who was twenty-eight and already a highly respected gynaecologist. He had a wild sense of humour which Alicia warned him to repress in the presence of her parents, so to them he appeared a well-groomed young man of cheerful mien, on the way up in his profession.

Since Alicia was unmarried, Frick called on her before the married nurses, in case of emergency. It was almost the same for Geoff, since babies arrived at any hour, and Geoff said he had lost his biological time clock, if he had ever had one. Still, they managed to spend an evening or two a week together, and Geoff had a small apartment in town. Alicia told Geoff about the Reverend Townsend's remark about surrogate mothers' commercialism, when they met for a coffee in the Frick canteen.

'Commercial – at ten thousand plus medical expenses?' Geoff gave a laugh. 'I wouldn't do it for that. Maybe these Birdshitters think we're doing genetic engineering, creating a super-race. Ha-

ha! – Oh, that reminds me, a nurse told me Sarah Morley – Morgan, I forget the last name, lost her job in Cleveland because of this.'

'Because of what?'

'Because she was a surrogate mother once. Here. She's a Meadsville girl. Maybe she told another girl in the office who told the boss who's maybe a Birdshitter. Anyway she's short of money and needs another job – from us.' Geoff lifted his mug of black coffee and drank. 'I told the nurse to write back, sure, come around for the usual physical, and we'll try to set a date.'

Alicia didn't recall Sarah, but it didn't matter. All the surrogates were in their early twenties, healthy and fit-looking. They received, by a simple operation that required no anaesthetic, the in-vitro-fertilised egg that would become a baby. In a long lab room on the ground floor, where Geoff often worked and where Alicia went for blood test results, there were refrigerators for labelled eggs and sperm, incubators for fertilised eggs, and a room off the lab with a table, couch and TV, used by the lab technicians and the doctors for short breaks or a snooze. This room could be locked from the inside, Geoff said, and he had told her that this room was where the husbands went to 'produce', and that Frick had put some girly magazines on the table to inspire them, and that some men couldn't make it even on the third and fourth visit, which Geoff found amusing, though quite normal. 'Not sure I could either, under those circumstances!' Geoff had said with a guffaw. 'But it's a better atmosphere than these cabins I've heard about, with fellows lined up outside waiting their turn!' Geoff sat up taller. 'I'd better split. You still free for Tuesday night?'

Alicia smiled. 'What a memory! Yes!'

'See you!' Geoff's tall figure made for the canteen door, his unbuttoned white smock flying behind him.

On Tuesday evening, Alicia cooked dinner in Geoff's apartment, and afterwards they drove to a roadside bar and restaurant where there was dancing. Then back to Geoff's, where Alicia stayed the night. They talked about the house they intended to buy. Geoff had put down option money on it, and he expected to strike a bargain with the owner. It was a two-storey house, old enough to have personality, and on the side of town nearest the Frick.

Alicia had almost forgotten the surrogate mothers subject, when she received a letter from her old school friend Stephanie Adams, who lived about sixty miles away in another town, and was now married and expecting a baby, Alicia knew. Stephanie wrote that the company she worked for, Jebson Parts, was not going to give her her job back after a two-month maternity leave, as they had promised nearly a year ago, and that it was because Jebson had found out she had been a surrogate mother once.

. . . They brought it up, and I said yes, I had been, because I was broke. You'd think it was prostitution! And who's behind this? The old Mighty Right people, yacking away in churches against abortion, contraceptives for teenagers, etc. Why doesn't the Mighty Right attack prostitution which can spread AIDS, for instance, instead of lambasting the healthiest young women in the country? . . .

I'm in touch with about ten young women who've been surrogates, because every one of them seems to know another surrogate, maybe married and living somewhere else now. I heard from one in Florida that the powers that be are trying to lower our average fee of $10,000 plus expenses. And how? By stigmatising us as money-minded sluts, and/or paid slaves of 'the rich' who either can't accept God's will or are too lazy to bear their own kids. Switch on your radio or TV to one of these religious stations, Alicia, and you might get an earful . . .

So I and some of the girls are thinking of forming a union called Rent-a-Womb. Don't laugh, because we have to have a catchy name to get public attention. *Then* they can call us commercially-minded, if they want, but I bet we'll win if we address the nation! A fat lot the present administration cares about America's 'growing class of young and poor', as they call it in an article in today's paper . . .

When are you and Geoff tying the knot? Give him my best! George has sent off his novel to his New York agent with fingers crossed. And I'm expecting in three weeks exactly from now.

Love from your ol' pal
Steph

George Fuller, Stephanie's husband, was a writer and had had some short stories published but not yet a novel, Alicia remembered. Steph had been a surrogate mother during the time Alicia was in nurses' school. Geoff had delivered the baby, Steph had said, though at that time Alicia hadn't yet met Geoff. Without the surrogate mother's fee, Steph and George wouldn't have been able to marry, or at least not as soon as they had. The parents had been so delighted with their baby boy, they had given Steph a five-hundred-dollar bonus. George Fuller, a college graduate, had been doing carpentering and house-painting jobs in Meadsville then, and he still did such work, Steph had said in her letter. Now, with Steph's job gone, Alicia wondered how they were going to make ends meet.

Alicia told Geoff about Stephanie's letter at the next opportunity, which was around 3 one afternoon in the canteen. 'Isn't that hellish? She and George're living on a shoestring, anyway,' Alicia said. 'Remember Steph? Light brown hair, full of pep?'

'Of course I do!' Geoff had pushed his white head-cover back and it dangled at his neck. There was a spot or two of blood on one sleeve of his white gown. He had told Alicia that he had helped deliver two babies in the last hour. 'I remember her telling me she was surprised at how easy it was – having a baby. And that was her first.' Geoff smiled broadly. He had dark straight hair and a slender, neat moustache, which he thought made him look older, he had once told Alicia. 'So now she's forming a union. Good idea. – That reminds me. You know Mrs Wilkes, reddish hair, talks a lot?'

'Um-m. Yes, why?'

'She was admitted this morning early to emergency. Second miscarriage and she's pretty upset. When she's on her feet tomorrow, I'll suggest a surrogate. A national union's a good idea, then we'll have a list of names.'

'Calling Dr Geoffrey Robinson. Dr Robinson. Please go to Room Five Hundred and . . .'

Geoff had pushed his chair back. 'We still have a date this evening? Seven? Six?'

'I can make it at six with luck.'

'And I'll try. Look for me down in pre-natal.' He flew off.

Alicia and Geoff made the date, and drove in two cars to Geoff's apartment house.

Geoff made Bloody Marys. 'Hey, somebody left a flyer on the desk in pre-natal just now – about what you were talking about. I'll show you.' He went to his raincoat and took a yellow page from a pocket. 'This. Is that the church your folks go to?'

Alicia looked at the church's name in heavy black letters at the bottom of the page. 'No, glad to say.'

was the heading, followed by a verse from the Bible, which to Alicia
had nothing to do with the subject, and then a paragraph about
'hired mothers' attempting to organise 'in order to raise their fees
for their unnatural profession', from which 'certain hospitals' also
profited. She read on:

> ... Women's bodies are not factories, and babies are not objects
> manufactured like cars or aeroplanes. The union of man and wife is
> a holy one. Interference with God's and nature's way, in the
> conception and bearing of God's and nature's fruit, leads only to
> the misery and despair that come from awareness that one has
> broken God's faith in us his children.
>
> Our church is one of many which protest the exploitation of
> conception and birth. Speak to your spiritual leader in our or your
> local church. Let your voice be heard!

'Gosh,' Alicia said, 'they're even taking a crack at birth control.'
'Yes, and the bit about organising – '
'Steph told me a couple of the girls were journalists and had
already written some articles about Rent-a-Womb.'
'Good,' said Geoff, slumped in an armchair with his drink, while
Alicia was just as comfortable on the sofa with her feet up. 'Probably
more computers in Mighty Muck's headquarters than in the whole
Internal Revenue Service.'
The next day, when Alicia had the afternoon off and was home
by 1, her mother pointed to an item in the Meadsville *Sun*, and
asked Alicia if she had seen it. Alicia hadn't. It said:

SURROGATE MOTHERS FORM UNION

In response to what their organisers call harassment and attempts
to lower their unofficial fees, several former and present surrogate mothers have formed a union called Rent-a-Womb. Leaders
Mrs George Fuller and Frances Chalmers of Brookvale say they
have over 300 members from all over the nation and more are
joining daily. The young women have in the past received about
$10,000 as fee, plus expenses for medical care and, occasionally,
maternity clothing.
Rent-a-Womb says that certain 'wrongly informed' groups are

attempting to halt the practice of using substitute mothers in the case of inability of the true mother to conceive, or carry a baby to term, or infertility when the husband is not infertile, in which case the baby is conceived by artificial insemination of the surrogate. By stigmatising surrogates as 'something like call-girls or at best money-mad and inhuman, some groups are hoping to put us down'. The spokeswoman added, 'To be sure, most of us needed or need the money, but we also like children, and couldn't have got this work from reputable doctors unless we were healthy and normal. Hundreds of happy parents would not have been parents without us.' She said that these 'new parents' could help by speaking out against Rent-a-Womb's detractors.

'Well – ' Alicia began, because her mother was waiting.

'Not commercial? They'll be trying to raise their fees next. What else do unions do?'

'I *have* seen some happy parents, Mom. Just as it says here. Who's it harming?'

Her mother gave a cool smile. 'But to try to *organise* like this – so blatantly! – No doubt these union women are the same types who're pro-abortion-on-demand. Very rough types, I'd imagine. I have the feeling you're sympathetic to them.'

Alicia hesitated, aware that she still lived under her parents' roof. 'Consider me neutral, Mom. There're two sides to this. It's the married couples who *ask* for young women to bear their child.'

'But what kind of young woman would *do* this?'

'Usually poor girls, Mom. You think we haven't got poor people in the States? Lots of – ' Alicia hesitated, then plunged on. 'Some poor girls become prostitutes or variations thereof, because they're broke. It's not only young blacks who can't find a job, or who're short of money.'

Her mother winced. 'Whether people can have offspring is God and nature's business, dear Alicia, and not the heaviest burden to bear in life. Of course science can cross a chimpanzee with a goat, I suppose. But why do it?'

Alicia was silent. Her mother had played golf this morning. She was fit and trim and in her mid-forties, yet talking like Methuselah. Or Birdshall. It was usual for people like her parents to say that Birdshall was 'really *too* conservative', though at the same time they never contradicted anything Birdshall said. 'I'd call Birdshit a fossil,' Geoff had once said, 'but he doesn't believe in fossils. He thinks the world was created about ten thousand years ago, four thousand if he's got his steam up.'

'Rosemary told me this morning,' her mother went on, 'that the American Committee for Loving the Unwanted is planning a mass funeral for aborted foetuses in Los Angeles in a few days. They've collected bags of these foetuses from the back doors of hospitals and – '

'A funeral? You don't mean it, Mom!' Alicia interrupted. It struck her as satirical, like something she might read in *Mad* magazine.

'Of course I mean it. I've heard that hospitals usually throw these foetuses away as if they were garbage.'

'Then you've heard wrong, Mom, they're used,' Alicia said calmly. 'They're *very* useful for research – developing prophylactic medicines, for instance. They're not wasted.'

Mrs Newton looked blank with surprise. 'All the more horrid.'

The day after this conversation with her mother, Alicia had more news from Steph. The tone of her letter was excited, her writing full of abbreviations. She said Rent-a-Womb was growing by leaps and bounds, but so was opposition in the form of Birdshall's daily Bull.

. . . This self-appointed Pope manages to say something against us every day on TV and radio . . . We have to counter hard and fast, so my branch of Rent-a-Womb with 22 members is coming to Meadsville Fri. for a Sat. rally, because Birdshall is blasting nationwide Sunday. Most of the girls will be staying at Hotel Crown, accom. already OKed and 3 have trailers that can each sleep at least 2. I'm broke now from terrific postage, printing and phone expenses, so I wonder can you put me up for 2 nights, Fri. & Sat.? I'll be out except for sleeping. A personal appearance in my expanded state will help, I think: once a surrogate, now married and carrying my own child by my own husband! . . . Could you get a list of former surrogates at Frick, maybe from your swain Geoff. If there is no time before rally for me to contact all of them, the list will still be useful in future . . . Frances Chalmers is great, 22, journalist, has been a surrogate twice, and has small child of her own. She knows of a girl in San Antonio who accepted $8,000 as surrogate with no pre-natal paid for, and F. thinks something must be done. Her latest article appears Sat.

in local papers here, also *NY Times* & in a San Fran. paper. How about that?

Alicia showed Stephanie's letter to Geoff, and Geoff said he would get a Frick secretary to make the list Steph wanted.

'That's going to be interesting Saturday,' Geoff said. 'A Rent-a-Womb rally in Meadsville! Maybe here on the Frick grounds! Ha-ha! Plenty of room out on the lawn there. Maybe some Mighty Righters'll turn up too. Did your parents say anything?'

'Not yet.' Alicia as usual felt a bit ashamed of her parents' conservatism. 'Not sure if they know yet.'

Her parents knew by that evening. The Rent-a-Womb rally on Saturday was the first thing her mother informed Alicia of, when Alicia came in at 7. Her parents had heard it on the 6 o'clock news.

'The TV news even said that Frick had done at least thirty surrogate – operations or whatever you call this business,' Alicia's father put in.

Alicia had telephoned Stephanie from the Frick, and said of course Steph could stay in the guestroom Friday and Saturday nights. Alicia had found it impossible to say no to an old friend, and she knew she could arrange something with Geoff at his place, if her parents made a fuss. But her parents might not connect Stephanie Adams with Mrs George Fuller. Friday was tomorrow.

By arrangement with another friend, to whom Alicia promised to do a similar favour at some other time, Alicia took a few hours off on Friday afternoon, and met Stephanie at the bus terminal. Stephanie had a small suitcase and a larger rope-tied carton which held flyers and publicity material, she told Alicia, and Alicia at once took it from her to carry.

'Lovely to see you!' said Stephanie, pink-cheeked and beaming. 'And have I got news!'

They decided to have a coffee in a nearby diner before driving to the Newton house. Steph talked like a machinegun.

'Rent-a-Womb's the theme of Birdshall's Sunday sermon nationwide. We couldn't have asked for better advertising, couldn't have paid for a minute of it and he's giving us an hour! Supposed to be a secret but we found out. We have friends, Alicia, you'd be amazed . . . And how's Geoff? . . . You're looking fine, by the way, more than I can say for myself right now but my spirits are high! . . . Listen, what's your parents' attitude?'

Alicia told her. 'I'd better keep that carton in my room – which you can use, of course, too. I'm out a lot, and there's a telephone in my room, because I sometimes get calls from Frick at night. You see, my folks don't know you're Mrs George Fuller of Rent-a-Womb. I just said Steph was coming.'

'I see. Thanks, Alicia. You're a darling.' Steph chattered on. The Rent-a-Womb girls were already in Meadsville at the Crown or in their trailers, working on publicity for tomorrow. The girls intended to take some photos of Steph outside the Frick Medical Center, and they hoped that a couple of TV crews would turn up Saturday.

When they got to Alicia's house, Alicia's mother was home, and greeted Stephanie, whom Alicia called merely 'Stephanie'.

'Remember you? Of course I do!' said Mrs Newton, who was in dungarees and had been gardening. 'Wasn't all that long ago. Two years?'

'Something like that. A lot's happened, as you see. I'm married and expecting.'

'Bless you!' said Mrs Newton. 'Alicia, there've been two phone messages, one for you, one for Stephanie. I left the messages by the downstairs phone.'

'Thank you, Mom.'

Alicia took the slips of paper, and went with Stephanie up the stairs, carrying the carton which weighed over twenty pounds. Alicia's mother wanted to carry the little suitcase, but Stephanie thanked her and insisted on carrying it, saying it was good for her.

One message was from Geoff, to call him at 5:55 if she could, and the other from someone whose name Steph knew and who wanted Steph to call her at once at the Crown.

'One thing I must settle,' Stephanie said, groping in her handbag. 'I want to leave twenty dollars for my phone calls with your family. – No, no, it's only normal, Alicia! I'll feel awful if I don't. They'll all be local, I promise. If you don't take it, you'll make me have a miscarriage!' Stephanie cried, laughing.

Alicia reluctantly took the twenty-dollar bill.

Stephanie made her call from the telephone in Alicia's room, and promised to meet someone at the Crown in less than half an hour. Then it was five to 6, and Alicia phoned Geoff at the ground floor lab number, the one she knew he meant her to call.

Geoff himself answered. 'How's Steph? . . . Tell her the union girls have been here already, looking the grounds over for tomorrow's do. And did you know Mighty Muck's turning up tomorrow too? . . . What about your mom?'

'Okay so far. Steph said she'd be out a lot.'

'Aren't you on tonight? I'm here till midnight, the way it looks.'

'Nine to midnight Special Private,' Alicia replied. 'Third floor, you know?' She meant Geoff could leave a message with the Hall Attendant on the third floor.

Alicia went into the guestroom, where Stephanie had opened her suitcase and hung a dress in the closet. Stephanie washed her hands in the upstairs bathroom, and was ready to leave with a bundle of flyers from the carton, when Alicia's mother called from downstairs: 'Alicia? Can you come down for a minute?'

Alicia went down. Her mother drew her into the living-room, and said she had just had a telephone call from Rosemary who had told her that Stephanie Fuller was head of the Rent-a-Womb women.

'Is that *this* Stephanie?' asked her mother. 'Rosemary said she used to live in Meadsville.'

Alicia sighed. 'Yes, Mom. – And we'll take off. I mean – I'll see that Steph finds a place tonight.'

'I really can't, you know, Alicia? I can't put up people like that in my own house – even if they were once friends of yours.'

Alicia said nothing, not sulking, but she found nothing to say.

When she helped Stephanie down with her luggage, her mother was not in sight. Alicia drove Stephanie to the Crown, and said she was sure Geoff could let Stephanie have his place, or put her up in his place on a cot which he could easily borrow from the Frick.

'Or I can pile in with someone at the Crown,' Stephanie said cheerfully. 'The girls'll finance me for two nights. I should never have imposed myself – '

'Oh, can it, Steph! You, my best friend in highschool? And even before that? I'm sorry about my folks.'

'If you think *this* is a big deal! We've been screamed at and even hit by some women – and some men too. Tell your mother thanks, anyway, would you?'

Alicia remembered to give Steph her twenty dollars back. In the lobby of the Crown, Stephanie introduced Alicia to three or four Rent-a-Womb members. They were all friendly and smiling. One girl was pregnant. It struck Alicia that every one looked cleaner and healthier than the average young woman, but then they were healthier than the average, otherwise they couldn't have been surrogate mothers.

Steph had given Alicia four or five one-page flyers which Steph called their 'package', and which Rent-a-Womb members handed out at street corners. Some pages were Mimeographed, others printed. Alicia took a look at them in the Frick canteen, where she had decided to eat her dinner instead of going back to her parents' house. An orange-coloured flyer said:

WHY 'RENT-A-WOMB'?

After a nearly twenty-year record of healthy babies brought forth by surrogate mothers, and mutually agreed upon contracts between couples and surrogates, some groups within the United States see fit to try to halt surrogate services.

How? By a verbal campaign implying that our work is mercenary (true, most of us needed or need the money), immoral (how so?), damaging to family life (we are helping to create families), and damaging to the newborn who is taken away from its surrogate mother just after birth. Does anyone remember the seconds and hours just after being born?

The unofficial fee nationwide for surrogate mothers has been up to now around $10,000 plus medical expenses and sometimes partial financial support in the last weeks of pregnancy, if the jobs of girls were of a nature not to be performed in a state of advanced pregnancy.

Now certain churches, women's groups and indeed some men's are trying to stop surrogate mothers' services not by going to court and making a specific charge, but by, for instance, pressuring hospitals (to which they may have made donations that they now threaten to withhold or cease) to stop artificial (in-vitro) fertilisation. This is an attempt to turn surrogates into outlaws, willing to accept ever lower fees, while for married couples who want a baby, the whole procedure would become *more* expensive, if middlemen have to be paid. If anti-surrogate people have their way, hospital procedures will have to be done on the sly . . .

Alicia took the next flyer and skimmed.

WHAT'S IT ALL ABOUT?

Bringing healthy babies into the world . . . The attempt to stop us, to lower our fees, will result in:

1) making ours a backstreet activity or/and
2) a luxury, as is an abortion in nations or States where abortions are outlawed.

Oddly, the anti-abortion people are the ones screaming the most loudly against us. Has it occurred to them that Rent-a-Womb members are producing babies, not killing them?

Has it occurred to them to ask the opinion of several hundred happy parents? Meet some of us tomorrow from 10 a.m. onward on the Frick Medical Center's east side lawn!

Everyone welcome!

Alicia glanced at the canteen door. Geoff had promised to make a dash down if he could before 9 p.m. He was in the delivery room, so his arrival was a hundred percent uncertain. She looked at a yellow flyer called THE BRIGHT SIDE, a list of eight or ten couples whose first baby had been brought to them by a surrogate mother. The list had a homely and very real look to Alicia.

Charles and Edwina Nagel, 212 Chestnut St., Pittsfield, Mass. Son Chas. Jr. now 2½. 'We were childless. Now we're not.'

Felipe and Dora Ortega, 10 Cedar Heights Rd., Leacock, Mich. Daughter Josephine, 3. 'We are thankful and hope to have another from a surrogate as soon as we can afford to.'

'Hi!'

'Geoff! Hello! Look at all this stuff from Steph! Want me to get you a coffee?'

Geoff looked tired and he needed a shave, but he smiled and nodded, seized the flyers and began poring.

Alicia came back with black coffee. 'My mother refused to let Steph stay in the house.'

'What? – You're kidding!'

Alicia assured him she wasn't, and that Steph hadn't been dampened or even surprised by it.

'One of my patients in pre-natal this afternoon – ' Geoff spoke softly, and glanced at a nurse and an intern at a table near them, but they seemed absorbed in their own conversation, ' – told me the women of the town are "quite shocked by these Rent-a-Womb girls",' Geoff said on a prim note. 'And they intend to turn up tomorrow too, I gather.'

'Pity I'm on duty at ten,' Alicia said. 'I'll have to look out a window – if I can.'

'Funny, I've got three fellows coming tomorrow morning to produce. What a time for it! Mighty Muckers outside chanting "Abnormal" and "Contrary to nature!" Ha-ha!' Geoff writhed with mirth, wiped a tear from his eye, and downed the rest of his coffee. 'Bye, sweetie! Back to the blessed events!'

The next morning, Alicia had trouble finding a parking place for her car, because other cars had usurped the nurses' parking row, which was not so sacred as that of the doctors. There were three parked buses, and at least two more arriving. No use looking for Steph in all the confusion of people. The east lawn was covered with women and men, some with banners, shouting and yelling, policemen even, trying to direct people. Alicia hurried into the Frick and checked in at a few minutes before 10.

'Get them *out*! . . . Get them *out*!' That was the first chant Alicia heard through the closed windows of a room where she was inserting a tube into the vein of a patient's right arm. He was an elderly man, and this was a blood transfusion.

'Did that hurt?' she asked.

'Not a bit, thank you. What's all the commotion outside?'

Then came the taking of four patients' blood pressure. When she was washing her hands around 10:30, she opened a window to the bright October sunshine and looked out on to the east lawn.

Feminine voices rose to her ears, then a male voice boomed over a loud-speaker, *'Keep our country pure!'*

That was the Mighty Right with the amplifier.

'Listen to what we're fighting *for*. – Take a look at (words unintelligible) and let them speak!' That was one of the Rent-a-Womb girls, and the voice had come from near the big gold-on-purple streamer held by two young women at either end. The streamer said RENT-A-WOMB, and billowed forth and back in the wind. Buses and a lot of parked cars were honking their horns. Each side was trying to drown the other out, Alicia realised. The Rent-a-Wombers had a sort of podium or stage, Alicia was glad to see, because the opponents had a small grandstand, like a section of stadium seating, and a larger platform just below it. From this platform the man with the mike was bellowing.

'... American tradition ... God's gift of children ... being turned into an ugly commerce which you see here ...'

Alicia tore herself away and closed the window. Back to duty.

There must be more than six hundred people on the east lawn, she thought. Had her mother turned out too, maybe with her friend Rosemary?

When Alicia next had a chance to look out of a window, things had hotted up. Some middle-aged women seemed to be tussling with a group of younger Rent-a-Womb girls on the left side of the lawn. A nurse, smiling excitedly, joined Alicia. Her name was Mary Jane, as Alicia recalled.

'Up those church people. I mean *up!*' Mary Jane made a vulgar gesture which suddenly seemed highly comical to both. '*They've* got all the time in the world to turn out, sure! Moneyed bastards, too!'

Mary Jane was Irish, Alicia thought. Even so, she was pro-Rent-a-Womb and probably in favour of abortion on demand. They both laughed madly in sudden sisterhood, and slapped each other's shoulders.

'Did you see the TV?' Mary Jane drew Alicia toward the nurses' 'rest room' which had STAFF ONLY on its door. The TV here was on, and several nurses standing and sitting watched raptly, some laughing, others gleefully applauding. The screen showed two women face to face yelling at each other, and seemingly about to come to blows.

'Where's this?' Alicia asked.

'*Dallas!*' a couple of the nurses answered in unison. One added, 'We just saw Los Angeles! Wow! It's all over the country!'

'Wish I were down on the lawn,' Alicia said to Mary Jane. 'My best friend's head of Rent-a-Womb – practically. Stephanie Fuller.'

'Oh, yeah?' Mary Jane looked at Alicia with sudden admiration, almost. 'Hey, I heard Mighty Muck's going to – You know the foetus burial in LA? Well, Mighty Muck's – '

Mary Jane never finished, because they all heard the hall buzzer and had to move. Alicia had thought Mighty Muck was solely Geoff's term.

'... would like to introduce ...' Alicia heard as she strode down the hall. Surely that was Steph's voice – she hoped so – introducing some of the happy parents.

Alicia had a half-hour break and could have grabbed a sandwich, but she was more interested in the east lawn, where it seemed more people had gathered since she had last looked. She could see the 'happy parents', three couples standing in a row on the podium amid the Rent-a-Womb supporters, all laughing or smiling, perhaps at the difficulties of hearing anything, because at least two mikes seemed to be roaring from either side. The Mighty Right people, who had strung up their red-white-and-blue streamer, were playing 'Onward, Christian Soldiers' on some kind of portable player while from the Rent-a-Womb side Alicia thought she could recognise 'Alexander's Ragtime Band'.

'. . . to read you about Abraham and Sarah!' yelled a determined female voice. 'When Abraham *thought* Sarah was barren, he lay with Hagar . . .'

'Lay an egg!'

'. . . ask you for *silence*! The President is going to speak . . . about sixteen *thousand* aborted foetuses . . . not *forgotten*!'

Cheers from squawky elderly throats on the Mighty Right side, and 'Yay-hoos!' from Rent-a-Womb. Applause and laughter.

'. . . foetuses collected from hospitals that would have thrown these babies out like *garbage*,' droned the male voice, coming from a source Alicia could not see. '. . . Now the voice of our President . . . committed to loving the unwanted . . .'

'*We* want them!' screamed Rent-a-Womb, and clapped hands and yelled. 'Birth control! – That's the result of no *birth control*!'

This got some laughter from both sides.

'. . . at the burial of . . .' Much sputtering of the turned up loud-speaker, as the President's familiar voice said: 'Just as the terrible toll of *Gettysburg* can be traced to a tragic decision . . . so can these deaths we mourn . . .'

Alicia ran down. She had to get closer, had to be in it! She nearly bumped into Mary Jane and another nurse coming up the stairs, and said, 'Come on down! Can't you get off for a couple of minutes?' Alicia raced out into the sunlight toward the Rent-a-Womb side of the lawn, looking for Steph.

'. . . human beings . . . ruled outside the protection of the law by a court ruling which clashed with our deepest moral convictions . . .'

This was the President, sounding deadly earnest. '. . . From these innocent dead, let us take *increased devotion* to the cause of restoring the rights of the unborn . . .' Mad applause on the amplifier.

Some applause from Mighty Righters but not much, because they avidly waited for more from the President.

'What's abortion got to do with Gettysburg?' Alicia heard a woman ask a man standing beside her.

'Um – uh – Well, it is a little complicated, but I'll try to explain when we get home,' replied the man.

'Alicia! I'm over here!' This was Steph, waving, standing on something, otherwise Alicia couldn't have seen her in the crowd.

Alicia cut her way toward Steph, and her nurse's uniform and white cap helped. 'Hi, honey!'

'Hi! – Sylvia! Meet my friend Alicia Newton. And Sylvia's husband Jed.'

Alicia said hello. These were a pair of the happy parents, Steph explained.

'Do you know, we've had so many people asking us questions,' Steph went on to Alicia. 'Women who never get pregnant, though there's nothing the matter with them or their husbands. You know? They want to know how they can get in touch with a surrogate mother.'

'. . . *persistence*,' roared the amplifier over the noise of the murmuring crowd, 'is what allowed us to have a resting place today . . . for these little boys and girls . . .'

'Foetuses *still*?' yelled a man from somewhere, laughing.

'Not fair!' cried a woman among the Mighty Right. 'Bad taste! Turn that *off*!'

'No, it's part of the LA foetus burial!' yelled a girl.

Day and *night*, we're Mighty *Right*!
Day and *night*, we're Mighty *Right*!

The famous chant sounded determined, but only about a dozen voices had joined in.

'That wasn't the President talking!' croaked a woman.

'*No*, that last voice was somebody else at that sick funeral and you *deserve* it!' yelled a man on the Rent-a-Womb side, giving a kick to two youths in white sweaters from the Mighty Right who seemed to be trying to manhandle him. Then a girl and two young men plunged in to help the man being menaced by the two white sweaters.

'Day and *night* – outa my *sight!*' countered the Rent-a-Wombers. The new chant grew. 'Day and *night* – OUTA MY SIGHT!'

'Alicia!'

Alicia recognised the voice of her mother, saw her mother with upraised hand or finger several yards away, as if her mother were admonishing her or maybe warning her of danger, and at that instant at least twenty people surged between them from the hospital side of the lawn toward the street side. Several people got knocked off their feet. A couple of women screamed, then it was a free-for-all, and nobody spared the elderly on either side.

'Keep your cool! No rough stuff!' Stephanie yelled to the Rent-a-Womb side, raised her arms for attention, even tried to jump into the air, making Alicia wince, because Steph looked as if she carried a bushel basket beneath her raspberry-coloured woollen dress.

The town whistles went off for noon, police sirens screamed from nearby, and Stephanie screamed, all at the same time.

'Oh, Geoff!' Alicia yelled. '*Here!*' She had spotted him coming tentatively down the hospital's steps.

Geoff ran toward her, and his white gown parted with his speed. 'Good thing there's a hospital near! Ha-ha!' Geoff neatly dodged a tall young man who was falling backward on to the lawn, having been shoved by someone.

'I saw Steph a minute ago,' Alicia said, 'and now I can't find her. She shouldn't be in this fracas!'

She and Geoff were dodging swinging arms, and sidestepping people who might have walked backward into them. The police blew whistles and yelled for order. A few people had fallen, unconscious or stunned.

'Stretchers!' someone cried.

Stretchers were coming. Five or six interns hopped down the hospital steps with stretchers and first-aid kits.

'Hello, Alicia! I'm Frances, remember?' Frances had a bloody nose. 'We're trying to protect Steph. Come this way!'

Steph wasn't on the ground, but she looked in pain, and was being supported by a couple of Rent-a-Womb girls who were plainly trying to move her in the direction of the hospital but without much success because of the crowd. Geoff grasped the situation, and called to an intern whom he knew by name. 'This job's my department, I think,' Geoff said to Alicia.

Within seconds, Steph was being borne on a stretcher toward the hospital, and Frances and a couple of other Rent-a-Womb girls were walking alongside her. Alicia heard a couple of taunts from Mighty Righters, something about 'another factory baby there', but Alicia managed to put it out of her head. She wasn't even angry about it. She knew that Steph had stated publicly today that she was going to have 'her own' baby, and if certain people hadn't heard her, too bad.

'We've won! . . . We've won!'

'We've *won!*'

Which side was chanting that? Both sides. Which side had won? Which side would ever win, Alicia wondered as she crouched on the lawn, helping another nurse bathe a bad scrape on a woman's arm with disinfectant, getting a bandage ready. Many people were leaving the scene, which made the dozen or so fallen figures more visible. A few zealots on either side still shouted insults at one another. Glancing up from her next first-aid job, Alicia saw the Rent-a-Womb girls, some of whom Alicia now knew by sight, putting away their banner, picking up fallen flyers from the lawn.

When Alicia entered the hospital, walking alongside a scared young man with a cut on his forehead that was still bleeding, she realised that she didn't know how much time had passed since the chaos of noon. She got the boy on to a chair, took care of his cut, and assured him that he wouldn't need a stitch. Alicia found another nurse to take over and persuade the boy to lie down for a few minutes, and then she looked at her watch. Nearly half past 1! She had been thinking of Steph.

She went up to the fifth floor, where both delivery and pre-delivery rooms were, and got the Hall Attendant to inquire, because she wasn't supposed to barge into delivery.

At that instant, the delivery room door opened, and Geoff came into the hall. He opened his arms and laughed when he saw Alicia.

'It's a girl! Easiest birth I ever saw in my life!'

'She's really okay?'

'It'll be hard to hold her down. Ha-ha! How're things on the battlefield?'

Alicia was suddenly sick of the battlefield. Steph was fine and with a baby girl! Babies were what the whole fight was about, *wanted* babies, that was. And neither side had won, she remarked to Geoff, and Geoff agreed, because neither side had listened to the other.

'But both sides are happy, don't forget,' said Geoff. 'Mighty Right always thinks it's won. And Steph was telling me Rent-a-Womb got a lot of names and addresses of people who want babies, so she thinks Rent-a-Womb won.'

Alicia's mother had a black eye. Of all injuries not appropriate, Alicia thought, this was the worst, and it looked comical on her mother's face. The atmosphere was worse in the house, really intolerable, so Alicia eased herself out. All it meant was that she and Geoff married a little earlier than planned, and they concluded the house deal earlier, and moved in.

NO END IN SIGHT

S he lies now, certainly a hundred and ninety, some say two hundred and ten, and with no end in sight. She doesn't know Sunday from Wednesday, couldn't care less, has refused to wear her hearing aid for the past ninety or more years, flushed her false teeth down the toilet at least a century ago, causing the nursing home staff to have to grind her food for her ever since. Now she's spoon-fed three times a day, four if you count 'tea', and pees in bed in a diaper. Naomi's diapers have to be changed ten or more times in twenty-four hours, round the clock. The Old Homestead Nursing and Rest Home charges extra for their diaper-using guests.

Naomi can't or won't bother pushing a handy red-glowing electric button that hangs over the edge of her night-table, she just lets go. When it comes time to change the bed linen, which is twice a week, two nurses lift her to a nearby chair which has a hole in its seat and is called a commode. The nurses spread Naomi's gown in back, in case she is in a mood to relieve herself while they are remaking the bed. Two nurses lift Naomi with ease, because she doesn't weigh much, into a wheelchair twice a month, and she is rolled to the 'beauty parlour' down the corridor for a shampoo and set, manicure and pedicure. This costs seventy-four dollars. Her thin white hair looks like a puff of smoke, but still her scalp has to be washed, the hair fluffed to make it look more like hair, though Naomi hasn't asked for a mirror in decades, and couldn't see into it, if she did: Naomi deliberately broke her glasses many years ago in a fit of temper, and those being the fifth pair the nursing home had had made (at Naomi's account's expense, of course), the home did not have another pair made. Or maybe the optometrist demurred, remembering how disagreeable Naomi had been the last time he had tried to fit her with glasses.

But if a pair of specs had lain by Naomi's bedside lamp, would she have put them on? No. What was she 'seeing' with her eyes half shut, as they were most of the day and night? What was she seeing in the rare moments when they were more open? What was she remembering? Were childhood memories more vivid than the events of her mature years, as everyone said? Maybe. Naomi mumbled, talked to imaginary characters sometimes, but seldom could the nurses understand what she said, and who cared? Naomi didn't say anything funny about the people around her now, as she'd done a hundred years ago when she'd used to walk, assisted by a nurse usually, into the refectory for a meal. Generations of nurses had come and gone since then, and Naomi's bizarre and snide remarks, being airy things and unwritten, had not been handed down to the memory of the current nursing staff.

Naomi's only offspring, her son Stevey, had not been wealthy when he died, but he had left his all to his mother, some seventeen thousand dollars. Stevey had never married. Of course his small fortune, which he had invested as well as possible in Time Deposits and suchlike, had long ago run out. But such is the luck of people like Naomi, that she was bequeathed another small fortune from an uncle of Stevey on Stevey's father's side, and that had lasted incredibly long, though not as long as Naomi was lasting. But more later of the odd financial situation. Stevey has been dead for about a hundred and ten years. He had a normal span of life, and died before he was eighty.

There's a TV set in Naomi's room, and she used to stare at its blank, oyster-coloured screen for a few moments now and then, as if she were seeing something, would talk back to imagined personages in sitcoms, but no more. Stevey had bought the set for her when she was eighty (Naomi had been seventy-eight when she entered the Old Homestead), but as she grew more batty, the nurses had slipped the set out to other patients' rooms (charging the inmates for its use, of course), and when the set went on the blink finally, nobody had bothered fixing it, and it had been put back, kaput, in Naomi's room. In case any of her relatives turned up and remembered talk of a TV set and asked where it was, there it was. But Naomi's relatives – living, walking, visiting ones – had always been conspicuous for their absence.

The Old Homestead's administrative staff and the nurses male and female sometimes chuckled over Naomi Barton Markham. Close to two hundred, they said, if she was a day! And still going! No *reason* for her to die!

Nobody of Naomi's family had visited in a century, the story went. The uncle of Stevey had died without issue and, remembering his brother Eugene with admiration, had left what he had to Eugene's widow Naomi, whom he'd never met. Very kind of that uncle, as Naomi had married a second time to one Doug Villars, who had not been a great earner. Amazingly, Naomi's legacy had held out for sixty years or so against the marauding of the Old Homestead administration, the adding of 'special care' hours, and prescriptions for unnecessary items, the most absurd being Tums for the tummy, which Naomi did not at all need, but which the pharmacy was delighted to add to the list of items that she did need. It was a hell of a racket.

Naomi Barton Markham's room on the ground floor of the Old Homestead Nursing and Rest Home in southern Oklahoma was a small room with one window and a private bath, which Naomi had not set foot in since she had been about a hundred and twenty. The room held, besides Naomi's bed, a chair for visitors, a night-table with little bottles and a drinking glass with water in it, and on the floor near the bed a bedpan that the nurses were seldom in time to push under her, if the bedpan was needed during the times of diaper-changing.

Someone of the staff had remarked, 'Babies *are* a bore with wet diapers and all, and it doesn't last long, maybe just two years. But Naomi – it's been fifty years or so now.' Then later, 'It's been eighty – a *hundred* years now, hasn't it?' And a circle of nurses and maybe even a staff doctor or two would join in the laughter in the Old Homestead's round-the-clock cafeteria in the basement.

Some stories got passed on like folklore.

'When Naomi was eighty or ninety and quite lively, she used to creep at night from one room to the other, switching glasses of people's false teeth – or she'd flush 'em down the toilet! That's what I was told when I came to work here.'

This story had inspired laughter and tears of mirth in dozens of young nurses and doctors. It was true! They felt it in their bones, it was true!

And there were stories of Naomi going into the kitchen during that short period around 3 a.m., when the cooks weren't busy with something, and Naomi would pour the salt into the sugar containers and vice versa, pull the plugs on the deep-freezers, anything to be mischievous. It was a fact that Naomi had had to be confined to a big armchair for a period of several weeks, given sedatives, shortly after she had entered the Old Homestead, and any nurse could verify this, as it was on record. Some nurses had looked it up, then asked for shorter hours or more pay for caring for Naomi, because the Old Homestead was not supposed to be a loony bin.

The truth was, Naomi Barton Markham was insane, besides being senile, but insane in a way that no one could label, or define. Multiple infarcts of the brain? Why not? Good as anything, and it implied an insufficient supply of blood to the brain, a condition a couple of doctors had told Stevey that his mother had, as if that summed up and dismissed the variety of oddnesses that Naomi had displayed over the years. Whatever she had, it wasn't Alzheimer's.

Further truth was, Naomi had cursed out, since the age of seventeen or so, nearly everyone around her, abused them in one way or another. First her boyfriends, who of course hadn't been good enough for her; then her husband Eugene Markham, said to have had the patience of Job; then her second husband Doug Villars, who had had even more patience than Eugene (Naomi knew how to pick them), and finally Stevey, who had at first worshipped the ground his mother walked on, then turned against her in an emotional and Freudian sense (he hadn't been in love with her any longer, after the age of fourteen, say), but not in a filial or legal sense, for he had always written to her if they were apart, and had continued to pay her bills as long as his rather lonely life lasted.

And now – though the word now means nothing to Naomi – it's the year 2071. Naomi's TV set sits there, looking as antique as an Atwater Kent radio might have looked in 1980. The Old Homestead is still called that, though the building has been renovated a couple of times, and expanded too, because there are more and more old folks. Naomi is lucky in still another respect: she's not in pain, doesn't need morphine or even aspirin. Incredible. Doctors from far and wide have come to study her innards, thinking, wondering: 'Can this fabulous Naomi Barton Markham have the low metabolism of the reptile?'

No. Her metabolism is pretty low, to be sure, but she does not exactly hibernate. She just keeps cool, and needs thin blankets summer and winter. But there has been a slow change. Now she talks more, talks to non-existent figures in her room, as if she has visitors. She talks often in a baby voice, and with a somewhat southern accent. It has begun to disturb the staff.

'Where y'all *from?*' Naomi will ask. Then she may identify an old boyfriend called Ned, whom she teases.

Or she may address her own mother, whom she lies to, and with whom Naomi exhausts herself, or pretends to – gasping as if in exasperation at not making herself understood by her mother, whom she calls Mama.

Then there is husband Eugene, whom Naomi clearly wishes to avoid, evade, banging her bony white fist down on the bedsheets, and yelling at him to get out of her room.

All this sounds very funny, Naomi speaking without teeth. Or rather, it sounds funny for the first several weeks to the nurses, male and female, who come and go, bearing trays, taking away soiled diapers. Finally, nurses start manoeuvring to get out of service in Naomi's room.

'I really can't stand it, I just can't,' said a 24-year-old female nurse from Wisconsin, plump and hardy and engaged to be married within a few weeks. 'I don't believe any of what she's saying, but it gets under my skin.'

That was it, it got under people's skin. They couldn't believe Naomi Barton Markham, yet there she was before their eyes, mumbling now and then by day and by night, talking to people of the past with such eloquence, they seemed to be standing in the room!

'Ah didn't say that an' you *know* it,' Naomi would say softly and grimly between her toothless gums, and an incoming nurse might almost drop her tray.

Despite the repetition of this and similar phrases, the nurses and doctors would glance into corners of the room to see if anyone *was* there, which made them feel silly and consequently a bit annoyed.

So nurses pushed the room on to new staff coming in, or neglected Naomi slightly, the diaper situation became worse for the next nurse in charge, and inevitably there was a next nurse, because the Old Homestead wasn't a charity or state institution, and they did try to keep up standards.

Journalists from newspapers, accompanied by photographers, came sometimes to visit Naomi. The photographers could always get a ghostly shot of her pale, folded little face, propped up against white pillows. Most of the time, she refused even to mumble 'Hello', as if she sensed that by disappointing the journalists she could hurt them, show her power. Naomi was a nasty customer at heart.

Naomi had no proper birth certificate. The story went that she'd had one when she entered the Old Homestead Nursing and Rest Home, but had got hold of it somehow and destroyed it out of vanity. She had always claimed to be younger than she really was. So was she even older than two hundred and ten?

Oddly, the coming and going of journalists and photographers and curious doctors taking X-rays and metabolism tests made Naomi less rather than more real to the Old Homestead staff.

'She's sort of like a statue now. Do you know what I mean?' asked a nurse who was drinking coffee with a colleague. 'It's like taking pictures of a monument – somehow.'

'Washington Monument lying down!' said a male nurse, smiling. 'Very pale and glowing – ha-ha! But peeing and crapping all the same!'

'She does seem to glow sometimes, when you walk into her room and it's dark,' said a middle-aged nurse in a quiet voice.

'I've noticed that too!' a younger nurse piped up. 'Pale and sort of greenish, the glow – isn't it?'

Nobody liked Naomi. She didn't show much of herself now to be liked or not, but what little she did show wasn't liked. And so it had always been, for Naomi.

In the beginning, she had been a small-town girl of slightly more than usual prettiness, with some talent for dancing. She had not lacked for boyfriends, and married at twenty-two. By that time, she was dancing with a vaudeville group which played Chicago, St Louis, New Orleans and Philadelphia.

Naomi Barton was blonde, slender, pert, not much intellectually, because she hadn't gone to school after her mediocre highschool in a Tennessee town. But the man Naomi married was an ambitious and promising engineer aged thirty, Eugene Markham, madly in love with her, indeed smitten. For a time, their careers merged nicely, he doing consultant jobs in towns where Naomi had an engagement for a week or so. Naomi's career prospered. Eugene suggested to Naomi that she might aim for ballet, something more prestigious than what she was doing, which was chorus line with a few comedy acts.

'I'll get stage-fright,' said Naomi, wanting reassurance.

''Course you won't! We can afford ballet lessons! When do you want to start?'

She started lessons in Philadelphia, but just at this time, Naomi discovered that she was pregnant, and she didn't like that. It upset her.

It upset Eugene slightly, too. 'If it's only one month, or six weeks as you said – maybe you can get rid of it? Hot bath or something? I dunno.' Eugene really didn't know. It was early in the twentieth century and abortion by suction-pipe was not so well known as now, though very likely primitive peoples on faraway shores had been sucking out little unwanted embryos for hundreds if not thousands of years before the time of Naomi and Eugene.

Naomi tried hot baths plus gin, resulting in a red face for herself, much sweating, but no ensuing period. She tried a long brisk walk in Philadelphia which got her into a wrong part of town, whence she actually had to run, but still she didn't abort. At this point, Naomi became confused: she couldn't sign a new contract with her manager for the following six months, because she'd be heavy with child by then. Oddly, neither she nor Eugene thought of looking for a doctor who would perform an abortion.

'Well, let's have the child,' said Eugene, smiling. 'It's not the end of the world, darling! It just means an interruption in your career. Not even a long one. Let's cheer up. I love you, darling.' Eugene tried to kiss her, but she twisted away.

'You don't! You wanted me to get rid of our baby!' Naomi didn't weep, she wasn't loud or hysterical, she was simply determined.

Eugene could not convince her that he was not only resigned to circumstances, but even happy with them.

Naomi wanted a divorce.

Eugene was thoroughly surprised. '*Why* on earth?'

'Because you don't *want* our child and you don't *love* me!'

Naomi packed, and took a train to Memphis, where her mother then lived.

Eugene Markham followed his wife to Memphis on another train, managed to see her at her parents' house, and tried to persuade her not to seek a divorce. He failed, and spoke with her parents on the matter. Eugene spoke well and eloquently, but Naomi's parents (Eugene had been able to see them alone) took the stance that they considered 'modern and correct': parents should not interfere in the affairs of their offspring.

Naomi got the divorce on grounds of 'incompatibility', since there was no adultery or absence without tidings. The child, a boy, was born in the home of Naomi's parents, and Eugene's offer to pay the doctor's fee and other expenses relating to the birth was rejected by Naomi. Two or three weeks after the birth, Naomi resumed her vaudeville career (in Chicago now), and left the baby Stevey in the charge of her mother, Mrs Sarah Barton.

When Stevey was nearly four, Naomi married a man called Doug Villars, a year or so younger than herself, a simple but decent fellow with an accountant's qualification that enabled him to get a job almost anywhere. Up to now, Naomi had been able to get a job almost anywhere too, whether she worked with a troupe or not, but the picture was changing. Vaudeville was dying out, Naomi was nearing thirty, and she did not adjust to the times. As she declined in ability and fame, and consequently got fewer engagements, she fancied her reputation growing.

'It's the ordinary public that doesn't appreciate me,' she said to Doug. 'I should've stuck with my ballet lessons – as Eugene used to tell me. Eugene had *ideas*! He wasn't a bore like *you*!'

Doug Villars could be hurt to the quick by remarks like this. But Naomi made it up to him in bed. She knew on which side her bread was buttered, and where the butter came from, Doug's modest but dependable salary. Besides, she enjoyed bed. But most of all, she enjoyed her power in bed, that was to say, her ability to say yes or no as to sex.

The boy Stevey was emotionally close to his grandmother Sarah, since she had raised him from birth to the age of four, and Stevey and his grandmother corresponded faithfully after Naomi married Doug Villars and moved out of Sarah's house. At nine and ten, Stevey was in love with his mother, as many boys are at that age, but Stevey was more in love than most boys, for the reason that his mother was seldom home. She travelled on dancing tours sometimes, while he and his stepfather stayed home, cooking and doing for themselves, and dreaming of the pretty woman who wasn't there.

Inevitably, Stevey had a difficult time adjusting to girls of an appropriate age for him, when he was fourteen and fifteen. He was supposed to be 'interested' in girls of fourteen and then sixteen and so on, he realised, but they struck him as silly children. He liked 'older women' of twenty and twenty-two, a few of whom he was able to meet, but who wouldn't have given him the time of day, he knew, he being only sixteen or so. He had no strong desire to leap into bed with them, he simply adored them, worshipped them from afar, even women aged thirty. A great reader, he was acquainted with his own syndrome by the time he was fifteen: he liked older women, and needed a mother, or a motherly type, according to Freud.

Stevey became an electrician, and did not waste much time pondering his personal hangups. He realised with faint horror that his mother was losing her mind – that was to say that by the time Stevey was twenty or so, he realised it. Stevey had left home after finishing technical school, and had lived in California, Florida and Alabama, but he kept in touch with his mother and stepfather, and visited them sometimes at Christmas. Stevey was also on good terms with his father Eugene Markham, kept in touch by an occasional letter, but Eugene had maintained a polite distance after Naomi's second marriage, which Stevey thought only natural under the circumstances. Then Doug Villars developed leukaemia. Doug had some insurance, but his lingering and fatal illness ate up a lot of the couple's savings. After Doug died, Naomi 'couldn't cope', as the textbooks put it. She'd leave something burning on the stove. She neglected her dog and cat till they were ill-nourished and flea-ridden, and her house was a mess. The neighbours complained (Naomi lived in a small bungalow in northern Oklahoma at that time), and the authorities stepped in.

Stevey was informed of this, and at once went to Oklahoma, was appalled by the state of his mother's house, and by her mental deterioration too. She didn't want to go to 'a home', she said, but Stevey knew that he couldn't take his mother in under his own roof. She was apparently staying up half the night, prowling the house like a demented wolf, poring over old and disorderly papers which she didn't want touched. A classic case. With some difficulty, Stevey got his mother into the Old Homestead Nursing and Rest Home (she had to be confined in a padded cell for a few days there, and no other nursing home in the region had been willing even to try to take her on), paid for her house to be cleaned up, then sold it at the best price he could get. The resulting money he put on deposit to earn interest, as he foresaw a long stretch in the Old Homestead for his mother, and how right he was.

Stevey Markham wrote to his mother a couple of times, but got only one letter from her in return. She had not liked him, she wrote, for putting her into a 'silly nursing home for old people'. Why couldn't he have let her stay at home, where she had been comfortable and independent? Stevey knew his mother well enough to realise that she wanted to start an epistolary argument, back and forth. So Stevey stopped writing to his mother, and within months, she stopped too. He visited her a few times, maybe five in all, starting with Christmases, of course. But Naomi usually chose to be huffy, to reproach him for not having visited her more often. And on the fourth or maybe fifth visit, she'd feigned indifference, looking at the ceiling, as if she couldn't bear the sight of him or the presents he had brought her. She refused to speak to him, and in this Stevey recognised her old joy in hurting him, or trying to. So he gave up these visits.

Naomi's upkeep cost Stevey more than his own in the last decade of his life, as her money (really that of Doug plus the money from the sale of her house) had run out. Then as if to 'save' Stevey, the remote uncle, his father's brother, had died and bequeathed several thousand to Naomi, simply because she had been the wife of his brother Eugene. It was, Stevey thought, a minor miracle: his mother could keep going for at least another twenty years (he knew how to calculate Time Deposits and interest by now, even without a pencil), whereas Stevey couldn't say the same about himself. Broke and seventy-four, Stevey was winding down like an old clock, and he died in his sleep of a heart attack, though he had not been overweight and had been a non-smoker. Stevey Markham had never had a proper vacation in his life. Shortly before his death, an odd thought had come to Stevey: his mother Naomi had managed to be a torture to others, a pain in the neck, even before he, Stevey, was born, by insisting on a divorce that his father had not wanted, but had agreed to, so that Stevey had been born into a fatherless home; and during his childhood his mother had picked quarrels with his stepfather Doug Villars, making their home life worse than rocky; and after Stevey's death, Naomi would continue to be a pain and an expense – to *somebody*. The State, perhaps, Oklahoma? The state with a small s, meaning the government? The Old Homestead would shunt her into something cheaper, once his uncle's money ran out. There were a lot of state-run institutions that were cheaper.

Before, during, and after, thought Stevey, as he composed himself for sleep on the last night of his life, his mother had been a trial and tribulation to all around her, had made good men weep, had made her son weep. And she lived on.

But by the time the uncle's money had run out, Naomi had become a curiosity. And people pay for curiosities. Sometimes.

Oh, yes, Naomi lives on. And she glows in the night, people say.

She mumbles, 'I'll *kill* you!' And then laughs, feebly, toothlessly. As if to say, 'I don't mean it, really.' For Naomi still senses on which side her bread is buttered, knows that without those fuzzy forms which are nurse-forms, which Naomi can barely see, she'd croak, die of thirst and hunger. So Naomi remembers to butter them up a little. But no more than necessary. In fact, she's as nasty to them as she dares be, tipping her soup over deliberately sometimes. Vaguely, she realises that the nurses are paid slaves, that they're obliged to hang around.

She gives the nurses the creeps.

The nurses, male and female, laugh, chuckle. But they chuckle defensively. They wonder, in the back of their minds, 'Is this crazy Naomi stronger than all of us, than any of us, after all? Is she really going to live for ever? – Because she's sure as hell around two hundred right now!' But they don't dare utter these questions, these ideas, even when they're alone with only one other colleague. There's something about Naomi that gives them the creeps way down deep, inside all of them. It's as if Naomi, somehow, could show them what life and death is all about. And that picture is not pretty, so they, and everybody, are, is, afraid to look at it.

They all shiver, the staff, because they know that all over the United States, all over 'the civilised world' where they don't push the old folks over cliffs any more, that the aged outnumber the young. In fact, it's the mark of a First World and first-rate country to have cut the birthrate to zero and to take care of its elderly.

So be it. And maybe it's the right thing to do. But people like Naomi are a horror. Their children will break themselves financially to keep such people *out* of their own homes and in some institution, where they don't have to look at them daily. The people footing the bills know they're being ripped off by the institutions, if they're private and not state institutions, because there's so much money in keeping these elderly alive with vitamins and antibiotics all the time and an oxygen machine when necessary. Not like in the state places, where a window slightly open on a cold winter's night can carry off half a roomful of non-paying guests with pneumonia – *poof*! So much the better, there're plenty more elderly waiting to take their places, and plenty of younger people heaving a sigh of relief at getting their parents out of the house and out of sight.

'She's a horror! I can't *face* it!' said one young nurse on Naomi-duty, shoulders collapsing from tears and emotional upset.

Well, the young nurse was given a day off. She recovered after some extra sleep and returned. And, like many others, tried to avoid Naomi, tried to attend the younger inmates, those around a hundred years old. Some of them were still willing to wear their hearing aids and dentures, a blessing to the staff.

It's 2090 now, and Naomi's certainly a little over two hundred years old. She glows pale yellowish-green in the dark, eats and drinks hardly anything worth mentioning, yet pees several times and defecates usually once a day. That's a sign that Naomi Barton Markham's alive, isn't it? Those wet and nasty, stinking diapers! Naomi started life in diapers, like all of us, and she is ending it in diapers, that is if there ever is an end, but there's no end in sight, really. Her 'condition' is unchanged in the last hundred and ten years. Her bill has gone up from about $2,100 a month at the end of the twentieth century to about $6,300 now, but the Old Homestead pays it, because Naomi is such a good advertisement for them.

The newspapers can ring up and make a date for fresh photos of the old ghost and 'an interview' any time they wish, but the articles are getting so old hat, Naomi's good for a story only once a lustrum now.

However, Naomi does serve as a symbol of the remodelled Old Homestead's and other private nursing homes' competence:

LOOK WHAT A FINE NURSING HOME CAN DO –
KEEP YOUR LOVED ONE ALIVE FOR EVER!

Never mind that 'for ever' might be an exaggeration. Who's going to point that out? No one dies any more, one passes away. Sounds nicer. Death is a word to be avoided. The old casket spiel goes: buy not only a satin-lined steel casket but a *double*-steel casket. It'll keep your loved one longer in a presumably lovely state, with the undertaker's cosmetic rouge visible on dead cheeks and lips for maybe three, four, five hundred years (or so it is implied, and how long would you ask for right out?), and double-steel will presumably keep the worms out longer too, though of course one mustn't use the word worms, or even think of, much less mention, the fact that worms come from those old fly eggs already within us, not from outer atmosphere or outer space, so expensive steel isn't going to help one damn against the fate that's in store for all of us.

However, back to America's private rest homes' pitch: don't you want your loved one or ones to live as long as possible? And in the greatest comfort that you can afford? Or even can't quite afford?

If other people are looking and listening, you'd better answer, 'Yes, of course.'

But if people aren't looking and listening, would you really want this? Would you want your mother or father to live 'as long as possible'? Don't you know in your bones that there's a time for each and every one of us to die?

Would you want your Mom to live on and on like Naomi, glowing green-yellow in the night, peeing in a diaper, defecating at least once in two days, dependent upon someone to poke food into her mouth, dependent upon someone to change the diaper? And with no end in sight? Would you like to live on like that, unable to watch TV, unable to hear, unable to walk even with a bit of assistance, unable to read a letter that an old friend might send, indeed too far gone in the head to take in anything that someone else might read to you?

Naomi Barton Markham glows in the night, and peoples her lonely cubicle with figures from the past, people long dead, more ghostly than herself – her own parents, her ill-treated boyfriends, her neglected but faithful-to-the-last son, her kicked around spouses (two). She curses them, mocks them and laughs at them, attempts with her minimal strength to sneer and turn her face away, as in the old days, as she once did to men who loved her, even to friends who tried to be friends.

You'll finish us all, Naomi. If not you personally, then your ilk. You're a triumph of modern medicine, vitamins, antibiotics and all that. Pity you can't pay for it yourself, but we know you don't give a moment's thought to that. You're light years away from thought, reasoning and economics.

Lucky you, Naomi! That is, if you're enjoying yourself. Are you? How does this incubus feel, lying on its back with a rubber ring under the rump to avoid bedsores? What does it think about? Does it go *gubbah-gubbah-gubbah* with toothless gums, as it did in babyhood, when it was also swathed at the loins in a diaper?

Naomi Barton Markham, you'll bury us all, as long as there's an old Homestead to rake in the shekels, as long as there's a fool or two to pay them.

SIXTUS VI, POPE OF THE RED SLIPPER

Pope Sixtus VI stubbed his toe badly on the morning of his departure for Central and South America. He had been in sandals on his way to early prayer in a subterranean chapel of the Vatican, climbing the four stone steps that he had climbed a thousand times before, when his right great toe struck the top step, and he would have fallen, if not for Father Stephen darting forward and catching one of his arms firmly. Sixtus had tried to smile, the pain was rather bad, and he and Stephen had gone on to the chapel.

By 9:30, when the Pope and his entourage were boarding the Vatican jet, the toe had turned bright pink and was throbbing. It was also alarmingly swollen, and Sixtus had made a change of foot-gear at the last minute: roomier black slippers instead of the snugger white ones that went with his light-coloured robe. It was June, and quite warm and muggy in Rome. Sixtus's physician Dr Franco Maggini had looked at the toe, made Sixtus soak it in what he called 'a warm astringent' while he ate his breakfast, but Sixtus failed to see that the soaking had done any good. There was even a purple hue, perhaps caused by bruised capillaries, over the end of the toe.

But at the door of the aircraft, Sixtus turned and raised an arm and smiled, as he always did, to the few hundred screened and chosen who stood behind a rope at the edge of the tarmac.

A small roar, cheers, cries of 'Santo Sisto!' went up from them. *'Buon' viaggio!'*

'Bless you!' Sixtus VI called back. 'God be with you!'

Then Sixtus settled into his wide and comfortable seat, fastened his seat belt, and accepted a small cup of tea that his waiter Giorgio brought him on a tray, because Giorgio would have been disappointed if he had not accepted it.

'Your Holiness is looking well today,' said Giorgio.

Was he? Across the aisle, he exchanged a smile with Stephen, the young Canadian priest who had recently been ordained, and whom the Pope liked to talk with, because Stephen was interested in politics as well as theology. Young Stephen was conservative.

Now *politics*. Politics was the reason he was making this trip today, his second trip to South America within nine months, though this time he would be visiting different countries. This time it would be Mexico City, then Colombia, then poverty-stricken Peru, then Chile where the government wore a uniform and people disappeared. Everywhere there was restlessness, dissatisfaction and unhappiness. Sixtus VI was very aware of that, aware that it was difficult if not impossible to look a hungry man in the eye and say, 'Trust in God and all will be well.' That was nearly as bad as the old admonition, the old cliché, 'Bear your hardships on this earth, and if you believe, you will live in heaven for ever after you die.' People were losing faith that a heaven or hell existed, even that there was a life after death.

The revving engines had begun to roar, the plane moved forward, pressing Sixtus's back hard against his seat.

Then they were airborne, and the Pope reached at once for the polished black leather briefcase on the table before him. He unsnapped his seat belt, though the craft still climbed. He pulled out the five-page address which he was to make in Mexico City at high noon Mexican time, a day or so from now.

'. . . God's word is unfailing,' Sixtus read, 'and He watches us all, neglecting not a soul. But there are elements in our midst today which seek to tear down this great structure of spiritual strength, comfort and truth. They offer instead a diluted and contaminated Christianity, one which tempts and appeals at first glance, but which is deceptive and hollow . . . First and always, absolute faith and absolute obedience . . .'

Sixtus's eyelids trembled with the pain of his toe, his own words before him became abstract, hard to hold on to. Yesterday when he had gone over the speech aloud, registered it and played it back to himself, it had seemed strong, truthful and also simple. The Pope admired simplicity: he often addressed unlettered people. Simplicity meant truthfulness to Sixtus, which was to say that a dishonest man speaking simple words would not be able to hide his dishonesty. But should he re-think some of what he had written here? He certainly had time, but it was hard to think with the pain in his right great toe, now quite as bad as a toothache.

'Your Holiness – ' Dr Maggini appeared at his side, bending, smiling. 'And how goes the toe?'

'I was about to send for you, Franco. It's awful, my toe. I've had only two aspirins, so how about another? Or something stronger?'

'*That* bad?' Franco's heavy brows came together, he rubbed his chin. He was about forty-five, with a neat but full moustache, fond of wearing dark suits even in summer, and now he wore a lightweight, nearly black poplin suit with a white shirt and dark blue tie. 'May I see it again?'

The Pope reached down and pushed off his slipper, his white stocking stopped below the knee with elastic top, and he pushed this down, and the doctor pulled it off. Stephen had got up and was somewhere else in the aircraft, though by now he knew Stephen so well, he would not have minded if Stephen saw his toe.

'You see, it's more swollen,' said the Pope. 'And look at that touch of *purple*. – What can that mean?'

The doctor was frowning at the toe as if he had never seen anything like it.

'You don't think it's broken, perhaps?'

'Doubt it, if you just stubbed it, Your Holiness.'

'Or out of joint?'

'Also unlikely. I believe the flesh – and of course the bone were badly bruised against that stone. Bone bruises take time.'

'But – ' the pain made sweat break out suddenly on Sixtus's forehead, ' – the swelling *is* so painful, it occurred to me that a lancing wouldn't be amiss. Couldn't hurt worse than this does now.'

The doctor shook his thoughtful head. 'But not yet, Your Holiness, a lancing might create complications. – Perhaps an X-ray in Dallas-Fort Worth.'

To Sixtus's annoyance, the doctor always spoke of the airport as if it were a single city. 'Or New York which is sooner?'

'New York is for refuelling, if you recall, Your Holiness, so security is not arranged. We're simply stopping at Kennedy for a couple of hours.'

Sixtus did remember. And the tour had to be on schedule, everywhere.

Dr Maggini gave him two aspirins from a box he had in his pocket. 'I would recommend that Your Holiness lie down and keep the right foot elevated.'

Sixtus VI retired to his private compartment. Here he had a wide bed, though not so wide as a *matrimoniale*, a shower, basin and toilet, a table with seats for two by a window. The bed could be curtained off, which Sixtus thought a bit absurd. Was this in case he died in the air? A little privacy for his final moments?

He lay down, propped his head against pillows, and looked again at his speech. But now, perhaps because of the aspirins, he felt sleepy, and he shut his eyes. The aircraft's motors made a sedating hum. He awakened from a sharp pain in his toe, as if Franco had indeed lanced it. But no. Franco was not here, and the throbbing was now like a hammer on a nerve. Sixtus blinked with the pain, alarmed. *I am mortal after all*, were the words that went through his head, but he had always known that, often said it in his speeches. He was but a human bridge between God and man, nothing more. Suppose blood poisoning, somehow, crept up his leg? Amputation? Well and good. Not fatal.

Why was the pain so awful? Sixtus started to press the bell for Franco, then drew his hand back. He was suffering, *this* was suffering, and how many times had he enjoined his people to bear sufferings of various kinds? It ill behooved him to whimper about a stubbed toe!

The Pope lunched with Stephen, Dr Franco Maggini and Cardinal Ricci. The atmosphere was cheerful, despite polite commiserations from the Cardinal about his toe.

'Things will go well,' was the attitude at the table, and Cardinal Ricci actually said it.

There was no X-ray laid on at Dallas or Fort Worth, and the Pope did not complain lest he run into 'no security' again. More refuelling, then on toward Mexico City. The Pope slept badly, and concentrated on, as he put it in his own mind, making a good show tomorrow. That was to say, doing his duty well.

Pope Sixtus VI had been born Luciano Emilio Padroni in a poor region of Tuscany. In a curious way, poverty, sadness and deaths in the family, hardship, and his fondness for Padre Basilio in his village had steered him toward the Church. After some youthful escapades, when Luciano had been nineteen and again at twenty-two, he had found his feet, and his feet were firmly in the Church. Luciano believed in God and Christ. He was strong in physique, fond of hiking and skiing, even now in his late fifties. He made friends easily, though he was not gifted with an aptitude for scheming. The public seemed to like his directness and his face. This had been so when he was much younger, but still it had been a surprise for Luciano, just years ago bishop in an unimportant Tuscan diocese, to be elected Pope. He had telephoned his mother, moments after learning the news. That had been six years ago. It seemed to him that the world had been quieter then, that nations had not everywhere been at one another's throats, but probably that wasn't so. The world did *not* change drastically, just became 'more so' in certain departments. Now it was the pro-birth control people again, flaring up in the United States as they had a few years back in Ireland. Bishops and priests in America had come out in their own churches in favour of birth control, in favour of condoning homosexuality and calling it a psychological aberration rather than a vice. Sexual intercourse before marriage was all right with them too. And equal standing in the Church after a second marriage. There was no end to these liberals' ideas, it seemed, and they did not realise that they were not making the Church any stronger by their new 'principles', but turning the Church into a leaky vessel.

Luciano Emilio Padroni groaned and tossed, unable to sleep.

Now in Mexico and elsewhere it was liberal theology, priests dressed like peasants, some even ready to fight with guns, agitating for land re-distribution, higher wages, all disturbing, all *irrelevant* to the meaning and function of the Roman Catholic Church upon this earth!

Luciano had thought he was awake, but the sun of Mexico really awakened him, golden and hot through the round windows of the jet as he showered and shaved himself, and dressed. By now he had to walk on the heel of his right foot. The swelling of his great toe had made the skin shiny, made the nail look absurdly small, like a button holding down a pillow. And the pink had deepened.

'So – a lancing now, perhaps?' Sixtus said to Franco as they breakfasted in Sixtus's compartment. The doctor had asked to see the toe, so here it was, stockingless, though the rest of the Pope was clad.

Again Franco shook his head. 'If it breaks, we have penicillin powder. I hesitated yesterday between an ice pack and simply elevating it.'

And gave only a couple of aspirins against the pain, thought the Pope. But politely, he said nothing.

Down the ramp now, as the crowd, held back by a three-deep wall of police and soldiers, lifted their voices in greeting. The Pope raised his arms, smiled, and once on the tarmac, bent and kissed its surface, causing such pain in his toe that he dared hope it had ruptured, but he did not look down at his feet. He wore loosely fitting white slippers, white stockings, a white robe with gold embroidery, and a round white cap on the curve of his skull.

An entourage of motorcycles and black limousines bore the Pope and his group toward their destination, which was the sports stadium of the University of Mexico. Sixtus had been to Mexico before, but to bless a cathedral, not to make an address. The President of Mexico rode in the limousine with the Pope, smiling but looking uncomfortably warm in a morning suit with wing-collar and white tie. The air-conditioning in the limousine had broken down, the Pope overheard someone say in Spanish.

Guards, off-key trumpets, and an attempt at a solemn march by a military band. The heat was enough to wilt a camel. The Pope, with crosier in hand, climbed wooden steps to a wooden podium and faced the masses in the stadium. The hum of thousands rose to a roar. Those not already on their feet in the oval arena stood up from folding chairs, while those in the bleachers stood up also, yelling, waving sombreros, applauding, anything to make noise. Sixtus lifted his arms in vain for silence. The Mexicans thought his gesture was a greeting and greeted him back. It was often so. The Pope waited in good humour, or at least with a good-humoured look on his face. He watched a nimble, shirtsleeved policeman, not ten metres away from him and below him, club a thin dog in the ribs to get the dog off the scene. Many in the crowd were eating tacos, plain tortillas, roasted corn on the cob, and the whippet-like mongrel was after a crumb, and it was not the only dog, the Pope noticed. Two or three skin-and-bone strays had sneaked in and were being actively pursued and kicked at by the policemen.

Throb, throb went his toe, like the pulse in his temple. Sixtus felt sweat run down his sideburns on to his cheeks.

'My people!' he began in Spanish. 'In the name of God . . .' He knew it by heart in several languages. The faint breeze lifted the pages of his speech which lay before him on a rostrum, and beyond the rostrum was a ring of black microphones, and beyond that the masses of Mexicans, mainly men in shirtsleeves and sombreros, but there were a good many women and children too. He could see fathers holding up their small children here and there, so they could say later, 'My boy or girl saw the Pope!' Sixtus VI saw two men in raggedy clothing competing for a position directly before him. One family seemed to have at least six children, all appearing small from the Pope's view. A few women with heads covered in rebozos wiped tears from their eyes.

'Silence!' cried a man on the podium.

'Throw him *out!*' said a voice from below, and the Pope saw a thin fellow in white trousers and a T-shirt, a man of middle-age, being hit over the head once, twice with a policeman's baton, then dragged half-unconscious by another policeman from the scene. The man's T-shirt had peeled off, torn apart, and the Pope saw the man's ribs clearly, as he had seen those of the dog a moment before.

'Thief!' said a voice from somewhere. 'He was after money! Shame!'

'Silence! Shame!' The voice, from a faceless man below, reached the Pope's ears. Shame that anyone spoke while the Pope spoke?

'My people,' the Pope began again, speaking without his written speech. 'I have a special message for you.' Often had he said these words in Lima, Rome, Warsaw. 'Pay attention to your priests, your *padres* in your villages – men like Padre Felipe!' Felipe in the State of Chiapas was the most 'liberal' and articulate of them all. The Pope heard a collective gasp, a single 'Hah!' of amazement from some throat below. 'Your priests are right to say that the rich are pitiless, that your wages are not enough – for human dignity or family nourishment. And too – '

The Pope had to stop, because a murmur passed over the crowd like a wind. Sixtus stamped his right foot, grasped his staff as hard as he could with his right hand, and set his jaw.

'Your Holiness – your *speech*! – Are you well?' It was Franco his doctor, bending anxiously toward him on his left, not daring to touch his left arm, it seemed, though his hand was outstretched to do so.

Sixtus VI felt suddenly angry at Franco, irrationally, insanely angry, and so he loftily ignored his doctor and continued. 'And *more!*' he shouted into the microphones. 'Since your poverty is a disgrace not to *you* but to those *richer* than you – you have every right, every conceivable right to try to improve your circumstances. – And you women, you mothers – it is not your duty or your God-assigned fate to be eternally bound to childbirth – as is a blindfolded ass to a wheel at a well.'

Sixtus paused, noticing curious stirrings in the populace before him. He sensed a storm coming, but sensed also that he had got his message across. Some figures below lifted their arms, as if afraid to cry out though they wanted to. The Pope banged his crosier down. 'My word is truth – *my* word!' The butt of the crosier banged twice on the wooden floor. The Pope, though not looking down, was trying to hit his toe. Again with full strength he brought the crosier down, and this time struck his toe squarely.

The pain was acute and heat burst out all over him, then coolness came over his forehead and he smiled at the crowd before him.

'*Bless you!*' cried Sixtus VI. 'Bless you!' He raised his arms, his right hand still holding the crosier. The pain had drained from his toe, and his right foot felt pleasantly cool even.

'Your *Holiness!*' Stephen had sprung up beside him in his dark robe, white collar, his young face smiling. He shook his head in a puzzled way. 'Your foot!' he said, pointing.

Now the crowd was on its feet and shouting, and there was too much noise for anyone to hear any definite words. The President and his aides gestured courteously to indicate that Sixtus should come down from the podium. The Pope knew what was next on the agenda: a visit to a certain plaza downtown and near the Zocalo.

'Is Padre Felipe in the city?' asked the Pope. 'I should like him with me today!' He had to shout to make himself heard, and he was addressing the aides, anyone rather than the President of whose co-operation he was not certain.

'*We'll* find Felipe!' Who had said that?

The Pope's right slipper was entirely red with blood, and Stephen pointed to it with an alarmed expression on his face.

The Pope made a gesture which said that all was well.

A limousine whisked the Pope, Stephen, Dr Maggini and one or two others of the Pope's staff, as well as the President, toward Mexico City. The Pope removed his slipper and set it on his knee. In the hot breeze that came through the partly open window, the slipper rapidly dried, and stiffened.

'Y-your Holiness,' the President of Mexico said, gulping with nervousness, 'I must strongly suggest that Your Holiness go directly to the airport. It is a matter of security.'

Sixtus VI had expected that. 'God's will be done. I am not afraid. The people expect me at the little plaza, do they not?'

The President, unable to contradict the Pope, nodded, bit his lip and looked away.

Padre Felipe had somehow got the message. The Pope saw his

slender, black-clad figure before the limousine had quite stopped at the plaza. Here were police and soldiers in abundance. The tall Felipe looked like a scarecrow as he turned this way and that with arms outstretched, quietly resisting the police who seemed to want to remove him from the scene.

'Felipe!' shouted the Pope, as he stepped out of the limousine. This was the 25-year-old Felipe Sainz, who had twice been in prison for leading strikes for better housing for field-workers and for clamouring too loudly for medical care for injured workers and pre-natal food allowances for their wives. The young priest looked astounded as Sixtus embraced him.

Soldiers and police gaped, and rather nervously watched the crowds all around them. They had more than a thousand people to deal with now, and more were coming via the many streets and lanes off the plaza. Here also was a podium or round stage, but of metal, like an old bandstand without its roof. The Pope climbed the steps with Felipe. Stephen followed.

'Your *foot*, Your Holiness!' cried Padre Felipe. He was unshaven as usual, with heavy moustache, ordinary dark trousers and tunic, which looked as if he had slept in them.

'My foot was hurting an hour ago, but no longer,' said Sixtus, smiling. The Pope's white stocking had also become red, but felt dry, as if the bleeding had stopped.

'This – ' Stephen turned the rigid red slipper between the finger-tips of his right hand.

Padre Felipe's eyes widened. 'Blood?'

The blood on the slipper had darkened, but its redness was unmistakably that of blood.

Sixtus VI placed the slipper at the edge of the rostrum, spread his arms, said the usual greeting and brief blessing, then picked up the slipper, which had its normal weight despite its colour.

'My blood – I am human like you – and mortal,' said Sixtus.

The crowd stared in surprise, puzzlement, many smiled, un-certain how to take the Pope's words, others stared with dark eyes into the Pope's face as if, by staring at the holy man at such close range, they could extract all the wisdom they needed to live.

Thus was born the phrase 'Pope of the Red Slipper'. Sixtus's stubbing of his toe (which he described) he called proof of the fallibility even of those in high office. The pain that had followed was a sign of error, and the relief of that pain, when facts were faced and dealt with, was truth, reality. A stubbed toe! That was a mistake that everyone could understand.

The Pope stepped to one side of the rostrum and extended his red-stockinged foot, so that as many as possible might see it. 'The pain is gone!'

Padre Felipe laughed softly, and his eyes sparkled.

As in the stadium, the somewhat stunned audience only slowly realised what the Pope was talking about, and why Padre Felipe was with him. The Pope extended a hand to Padre Felipe, and the priest took it. The Pope did not need to say more.

The low murmur of the crowd grew louder. From somewhere, churchbells began to ring, irregularly, sounding cheerful. A *mariachi* band started up tentatively in a nearby street, then gathered assurance and romped ahead. But mainly the crowd was solemnly happy, people chatted and laughed with one another. The Pope wandered among the throng, laying his hand for a few seconds on children's and babies' heads.

Policemen trailed him. The President watched tensely from where he stood near a row of black limousines. At least three television crews were at work.

A Mexican-style late midday meal was scheduled at the President's mansion. By now it was after 2. The Pope asked the President if he might invite Padre Felipe to the lunch? Or would that cause the President inconvenience? The Pope knew it would cause a stickiness, but hoped this would not preclude Felipe's presence, though the Pope did not say this.

The President, a fence-sitter of necessity, took a deep breath to reply, but Dr Maggini got the first word in.

'Your Holiness, I must take the soonest possible opportunity to check your temperature. In view of your foot – and the heat – '

Sixtus understood: the cautious doctor was trying to prepare an excuse for the Pope's words at the stadium and here in the plaza. *His Holiness did not mean everything he said. His mind was disturbed by a high fever at that time.* 'You may take my temperature, Franco, but I feel quite well, very well, in fact.'

'Your Holiness – may I suggest – ' The President sought for diplomatic words. 'The crowd is growing. The sooner we leave – '

The crowd was indeed growing, the soldiers and police had become more active, leaping into the air, brandishing batons. The gathering populace was cheerful, Sixtus saw, but the number of police and soldiers would soon not be enough to handle them. Cardinal Ricci consulted with the President, a limousine was pointed to, and the Pope was urged toward it.

They all got in, except Padre Felipe, to whom the Pope had to wave good-bye through the window. They were off, not to the Presidential mansion but to the airport. Half an hour later, the Pope sat in a chair in his air-conditioned quarters in the Vatican jet, with a thermometer in his mouth.

The good Dr Maggini had to concede that the Pope's temperature was normal. A servant had bathed the Pope's right foot in a basin of tepid water. The skin at the tip had split, but the colour and even the size of the great toe was back to nearly normal, and the narrow split was not even bleeding now.

'It's like a small miracle, isn't it?' said Sixtus, smiling at the doctor and at Cardinal Ricci and Stephen who were in the room with him. 'And where's my red slipper, Stephen?'

'Ah, yes, someone – ' Stephen began awkwardly. 'It could have been Padre Felipe, Your Holiness, though I feel sure he didn't intend to appropriate it, just carry it. There was some confusion in the last minutes.'

'A few moments in privacy, Your Holiness,' the Cardinal whispered.

The Pope made a gesture to indicate that he wished the room cleared. 'Go and have some lunch, my friends.'

Cardinal Ricci lingered. 'Your Holiness is perhaps aware of the consequences – '

'Yes, yes,' said Sixtus. 'It will take a while for my words to seep down to all the people – at their roots.'

'Seep *down*, Your Holiness! – Would you like to see the television now? Rome is broadcasting without stop. Ireland – New York, Paris. It's like an explosion of some sort. There'll be turmoil for weeks – longer – unless you temper your words, alter them a little.'

'Ireland – yes, I can imagine,' said Sixtus. 'And surely some people in America are happy?'

The Cardinal glanced at the closed door of the compartment, as if he feared a listener, or an intruder. 'Do you realise where we are, Your Holiness? On the tarmac in Mexico City. We can't go on to Bogotá. They won't have the facilities to protect you. No South American country can provide security – under these circumstances.'

The Pope understood. It was the friendly people who might crush him and his staff, not the men with guns who might come later. Surely the landowners were already busy collecting themselves. 'But to return to the Vatican now,' Sixtus began calmly, 'would look like a retreat, would it not, my dear Cardinal? Running for safety?'

'Why, yes, perhaps!' the Cardinal replied promptly. 'Except for the fact that the Curia is just as shocked as everyone else and not inclined to be – well, congratulatory, Your Holiness. I concede that our lives may not be in such danger in the Vatican.'

Sixtus told himself he could have expected the Curia to be chilly, even hostile, but the thought hadn't crossed his mind until now. 'Let's have some lunch and watch television. Or I shall,' said the Pope.

The Pope had a shower and put on fresh and comfortable clothes. He had made it clear to Cardinal Ricci and others of his staff that he wished to go on to Bogotá, Colombia, though their time of arrival might not be the time Bogotá expected him. Couldn't they spend the night on the tarmac here? Couldn't Mexican soldiers guard them, if need be? The Pope received evasive answers. The Cardinal promised to speak with 'authorities' by radio-telephone.

The Pope switched on the TV in his compartment during lunch with Stephen and Dr Maggini. He saw that he need not have worried about the loss of his red slipper.

The slipper with its slightly upturned toe, its simple slit as opening for the foot, had been duplicated a thousand-fold by now in Mexico, New York, even Rome! People had made slippers out of pieces of cardboard. The news announcer smiled and stammered as he explained the slippers in Spanish. Small children, grown-ups with tears running down their smiling faces, held up paper replicas of his slipper, coloured a bright blood-red. All this in less than four hours!

Sixtus caught Stephen's eye. 'I thought you would disapprove, Stephen, you the conservative.'

Stephen replied, 'It was the *way* you said it – especially at the little plaza.' He wet his lips nervously, though he was eating fresh papaya with pleasure, as was the Pope. 'I suddenly understood, Your Holiness.' Stephen glanced at the Cardinal and Dr Maggini, who were both watching the TV screen with rather long faces. 'You can count on me,' Stephen said softly.

'Thank you, dear Stephen. I mean to go on to Bogotá. – *I* should like to.' The implication was that he would not order anyone, not the pilot or anyone else to accompany him, because it now might mean endangering other people's lives.

'I shall go with you,' said Stephen. A moment later, looking at the TV screen, he said, 'These little slippers! Unfortunately, Your Holiness, by tomorrow they'll probably have them in *plastic*! Ha-ha!'

Now there was Ireland, Londonderry, a group of laughing women being interviewed.

'Bowled over? That we are! But it had to come, didn't it? We're all happy . . .' The voice-over began translating into Spanish. The Catholic women of Ireland were all faithful believers, and grateful to the Pope, one woman said, and would be even better Catholics for what Sixtus Sextus had done.

'Among the people, the picture in Latin American countries is similar,' the Spanish-speaking newscaster continued, as the screen showed a cathedral-backgrounded plaza that might have been in any one of scores of cities in South America. Men and women chanted 'Arriba Sisto!' while soldiers, mainly relaxed soldiers, looked on amicably with rifle straps over their shoulders.

The Pope with his remote control switched to another station, as his roast veal was brought in. This was a more serious programme altogether: an elderly statesman was being interviewed in Rome in Italian. Sixtus recognised him at once, since his face was as familiar as that of a close relative by now, Ernesto Cattari, head of a minority conservative party which never got anywhere in the Italian government, but none the less was important as a symbol of money, titles, stability of the Church, anti-Communism.

'. . . therefore we all hope that this curious statement is an aberration.' Here he gave a laugh in his short grey beard. 'A result of the torrid sunlight, perhaps – and best forgotten. – We await, of course, further comment from His Holiness.'

It was late in the evening in Rome, thought the Pope, and indeed Signor Cattari did look weary.

Madrid. Evening. The screen showed the façade of an apartment building in what the announcer called 'a rather poor working-class neighbourhood'. Women, a few men, leaned out of nearly every window, waving, smiling, yelling 'Arriba el Papa!' and 'Thanks be to the Pope!' A TV man with a mike in his hand spoke to a young woman on the pavement. 'You ask *me*?' she said in Spanish. 'I cannot find words – just yet. Except to say that Pope Sixtus's speech will change our lives – for the better, that's for sure.'

The Pope heard gunfire outside the aircraft some distance away, or so it sounded, and at the same time there was a knock at the door. One of the Pope's secretaries stuck his head in.

'Please excuse me, Your Holiness! We have just had an urgent request from the President – ' the secretary gulped ' – to leave the airport at once. The police are finding it difficult to restrain the crowds. People are *walking* to the airport – '

The Pope understood, and put his knife and fork down. 'Was that the shooting I heard? The police are shooting at them?'

'Probably only warning shots, Your Holiness, but as I understand, it is wisest to depart at once for – ' He stopped. 'The aircraft is well fuelled and ready for take-off, Your Holiness.'

'For where?'

'It would be best to go where we are not expected. We can ask permission in flight. Miami, Florida, for example.'

'I prefer Bogotá, as scheduled, though we're early. Ask if anyone wants to debark. To get off.'

'Get off the *plane*, Your Holiness?'

'You realise that it is dangerous,' said Sixtus, feeling that he said the obvious, but often it was necessary with his over-polite staff. 'Just ask. There must be time – a few minutes, are there not?'

The secretary disappeared.

The plane's engines started, its nose turned in another direction. The Pope switched the TV off. Out of a window he saw four, five male figures walking away with suitcases in hand. He didn't recognise any of them, but he didn't look closely. He smiled at Stephen.

'Bogotá. I shall send a message appealing for calm – dignity – thoughtfulness. A quiet celebration of the red slipper.'

The Pope did send such a message shortly after take-off, then closed his eyes in prayer and meditation in his comfortable chair. He had asked Stephen to interrupt him in case of important news, and had asked the Cardinal to report to Stephen. The Pope felt exhausted in a pleasant way and, if he dozed during his meditation, he would not reproach himself. Sometimes great ideas came in such moments, not to mention that he was going to need all his strength and ingenuity in the hours ahead.

Stephen awakened him with a soft, 'Your Holiness,' and handed him a folded piece of paper.

The Pope read: 'Respectfully advise not to proceed to Bogotá but return to Rome. Respectfully suggest revision of Mexico address be broadcast as soon as possible, or serious disorder can result.'

This was a telegram from several cardinals in Rome, all of whose names, six or seven, were at the bottom.

'A reply, Your Holiness?' asked Stephen, waiting.

'Yes, thank you, Stephen. Say, "Bogotá is scheduled. I shall fulfil my duty."'

The aircraft refuelled in Costa Rica. By then it was dark, 11 in the evening. The Pope saw a small crowd, hardly more than 'spectators' would number at any commercial airport. That was a good omen as to control. The aircraft's crew had negotiated in the preceding hour for refuelling in San José. Now they were due in Bogotá, Colombia, around 8 a.m. The craft lingered at San José, in no hurry. A mechanic stammered to someone on the jet that he was honoured to assist in the refuelling of Pope Sixtus's aircraft. The Pope heard this through an open door of the aeroplane.

Before dawn, a message came from a government official in Bogotá: 'We welcome the Most Holy Sixtus VI to our soil and will do our utmost to assure his safety.' It sounded a bit anxious to the Pope.

The crackling of gunfire blended with the hum of the aircraft's motors, as the jet landed at Bogotá's airport. A double ring of soldiers on foot faced the main buildings of the airport as the jet taxied. Floodlights had been turned on. The Pope saw an army tank or two and military transport vehicles at the airfield's edge. A message telephoned to the pilot politely requested the Vatican plane to wait with doors closed for security reasons, until further notice.

The Pope showered and breakfasted. It was just after 8:30 a.m., and there was no rush. By 11, he supposed, he would have given his address on the steps of a cathedral of the capital. The day promised strong bright sunshine. Dr Maggini came in to look at the Pope's toe. The split in the skin was closing and hardly pink any longer. Still, the doctor gave it another dash of penicillin powder.

At 11, a little later than promised by telephone, an armed guard arrived, escorting the President of Colombia, a sturdy man of about sixty with salt-and-pepper hair. He wore a white suit, and he greeted the Pope courteously, if tensely, after the Pope stepped off the gangway. The Pope smiled, then knelt and kissed the ground, rose and walked calmly toward the limousines which stood ready. These limousines had glass roofs, no doubt bullet-proof. Stephen, Cardinal Ricci and Dr Maggini were near the Pope.

'The people are very excited,' said the perspiring President after he and the Pope and the other men had settled themselves in one limousine.

'But happy, I trust. It is always so,' replied the Pope pleasantly.

A roar of human voices went up when the limousine came within a hundred yards of the cathedral. Here were walls of soldiers holding the crowd back, and helicopters circled and hovered, making a terrible din. How was he to make himself heard over the 'copters?

The Pope got out of the car. He sensed the crowds pressing toward him from beyond the barrier of soldiers.

'. . . Papa! . . . Sisto! . . . La zapatilla roja! Dónde *está* . . .' Where is the red slipper? they were demanding good-naturedly.

Sixtus smiled and raised both arms. 'Bless you! Bless you all in the name of the Lord!'

Slowly, then in a burst of colour, the red slippers came out. Children pulled folded red paper from their pockets. A row of teenagers unfolded a cloth slipper at least three metres long, and held it before themselves at waist level. All were laughing and chattering. Some soldiers who had been standing with linked arms got pushed to the ground, and they dragged other soldiers with them from both sides. There were shouts and threats then, in Spanish, which the Pope heard and understood. *Stand back, keep back or we must use batons.*

'Speak to our landlords, Sisto!' a man's voice shouted.

'Speak to our *bosses*!'

'My husband was killed by a soldier, Your Holiness! For growing . . .'

For growing cocoa? The Pope knew that a lot of Colombians grew cocoa for the cocaine industry, because otherwise they would not have enough money to eat. The matter was too complex to be addressed at the moment.

'My people!' the Pope began on the cathedral's stone steps. The people quietened down, but not the helicopters. The Pope turned toward the President, but spoke to a man nearer. 'These helicopters – '

'We regret! They may become necessary, Your Holiness! Security . . .'

'We want the Pope to come to our *fields*! Our *fields*!' This chant came from a sidestreet, and the Pope saw a couple of hundred – maybe more – men and boys advancing, their front men carrying a red slipper artifact a metre or so long above their heads. Soldiers blew whistles, and the military pointed their guns toward this advance from the sidestreet.

'Back! Keep *back*!' the soldiers yelled.

A helicopter dropped a canister which wobbled down, struck hard ground and sent up a cloud of whitish smoke. The crowd groaned disapproval at this. The soldiers yelled back. Sixtus saw soldiers level their rifles, not yet firing, but he saw nervousness in their shifting feet.

'I speak first to the women!' the Pope began strongly once more. 'Our mothers – our sisters – our beloved *wives*!'

Here the cheers seemed to rise to heaven, not only from the higher voices of women, but from men also.

'Women are not slaves but partners with men!' he shouted. Again the crowd yelled its agreement, and the Pope knew that he did not have to utter the words 'abortion' and 'birth control' for the populace to understand. 'Women are not slaves to their bodies either,' the Pope continued. 'Best if life is not created – if it is not wanted – if it cannot be fed and housed in decency.'

'*Olé!*' Applause and cheers.

The Pope sensed that his time for speaking was going to be short. The President was fairly pacing on one of the middle steps of the cathedral. Microphones boomed the Pope's words into sidestreets, and he could see ever more people advancing on foot toward the cathedral.

'I as your shepherd shall show the way!' the Pope went on, hoping for the best among those before him. 'There must be no violence! Our Saviour showed no violence! We must walk in his path, in *his* footsteps!' A little abstract, Sixtus realised, but the people responded, applauded with happy faces. The Pope had one last important message. 'Pay attention and listen to your *padres* – your priests – the ones who speak to you as man to man!'

That did it. Suddenly the scene was like a huge beehive of swirling, leaping figures, women who reached happy soprano notes, men with throaty cheers, and they knocked the soldiers down as they advanced. Sixtus saw a faint smile on the face of a soldier who had got a bloody nose.

'Your Holiness,' Stephen whispered quickly into the Pope's ear. 'So many people from the *outside* – coming – '

The President took courage. 'You will be crushed, Your Holiness, even inside the cathedral. We won't be able to keep the *doors* closed!'

And it was plain to the Pope that the President did not want the Pope to die on his soil for lack of security and protection. More canisters fell, and a few women screamed. Police began firing over the heads of the crowd. The objective was to make the oncomers halt, at least.

'It is best for Your Holiness to go to the airport! I am afraid for your life!' The President looked afraid for his own life too.

A hovering helicopter let down a plastic benchlike seat for two persons, with straps, and the President gestured for the Pope to get in.

'Stephen?' said Sixtus, gesturing to a seat.

'No, Your Holiness. Perhaps the President?' Stephen replied.

'There are *other* helicopters!' said the President. 'No problem! Do not delay!'

The Pope got into a seat alone, leaving the second seat empty, and fastened his belt. It was good theatre, he thought, like an assumption, almost, yet with considerably more danger, because he was still flesh and blood and mortal, and bullets were flying.

'To our *fields*! Our *fields*!' yelled a big group below.

Sixtus swung gently, gripped a seat arm with one hand and raised the other to salute the crowd. What a view! Faces turned up to him, smiling, staring, as if to fix the image of the Pope of the Red Slipper for ever in their memories. The Pope was slowly winched upward, into the body of the helicopter.

'Are we going to the fields? El Re Verde, perhaps?' the Pope asked. El Re Verde was a huge plantation of cocoa and coffee, much in the news because of the fact that workers had to be separated from their wives and children in order to be employed there, so vast was the land. Its cocoa production was said to be entirely for cocaine. A Colombia government agent of the anti-drug squad had been shot dead for trying to investigate El Re Verde.

'Not safe – El Re,' said the shy and embarrassed co-pilot. 'The owner does have a private bodyguard – army – it is true, but – ' The poor man did not know how to say no to the Pope.

'Let us go there,' said the Pope. 'You can let me down just as you picked me up.'

The co-pilot picked up a telephone. 'Reinforcements!' he said several times.

Word would get out quickly, the Pope supposed, that he was heading for El Re Verde. A soldier at the office with which the co-pilot was speaking would tell someone else and so on. A few minutes later, when the helicopter reached El Re Verde's fields, the Pope heard gunfire.

'It is not safe – Sire,' said the co-pilot. 'The *patrón* is firing on the – the workers now, because they are attacking.'

'Attacking?' The Pope could see fallen figures, perhaps six, on the ground between the low white buildings which surely were 'the headquarters' and a semi-circle of advancing peasants. Puffs, small clouds of smoke came from the white buildings, where soldiers or guards were apparently firing from the roofs.

'Can you let me down somewhere in the fields?' asked the Pope.

These were Sixtus VI's last words, except for 'Peace! Peace between brothers – in the name of the Lord Jesus Christ!' which he uttered as he stood for a few seconds on uneven but soft soil, among astounded peasants. Some of the workers carried sticks, some machetes, but the latter could have been for their work. All paused to look at him, this man, this Pope whom they recognised, descended from a Colombian army helicopter like a *deus ex machina*. They stopped advancing, yes, and their intention, one man said to the Pope, was 'to talk with *los patrónes* . . .' about their housing, their wages.

But the *patrónes* had guns, or their bodyguards had, and one bullet got the Pope in the throat. He lived for a minute or so, surrounded by shocked and chattering workers, whose group became a target for the gunmen in the company headquarters. A few workers lifted Sixtus up to carry him 'away', anywhere away from the main buildings whence came the firing. And as the word passed that the Pope had been hit, the *real* Pope of the Red Slipper, the peasants rallied, heedless of bullets, and stormed the main buildings, one of which was a fine hacienda-style two-storey house, where the *patrón*, his family and executives could work and sleep if need be.

The peasants' onslaught was met by a storm of bullets, many fired by machineguns. Not one of the peasants in the open field was left standing. But some at the edges got away to tell the tale.

From then on it was army and landowners against the people, and not merely in Bogotá, but in Mexico City, Chiapas, Lima, and in Chile's capital Santiago, where Sixtus had been due. Father Stephen got to Santiago, and quite on his own, as the Vatican jet returned to Rome the night of the Pope's assassination. Stephen was listened to: he had been at Sixtus's side in the Pope's last days, had touched the hem of his robe, as it were. Stephen preached over and over again, 'Peace – and discussion of all problems. Dignity of man and of woman too.' But the authorities did not like Father Stephen, and he was tolerated for a minimum of time (six hours), given no protection from over-loving crowds, except that volunteered by understanding and sympathetic policemen. Stephen had the definite idea that the leaders of this country would have been delighted if he had suffered the same fate as the Pope, but they hadn't had time to scrap the police guard, Stephen supposed. At any rate, Stephen boarded a Pan-Am aircraft and flew tourist class, safe and sound, toward Miami, Florida. He knew he was looked at askance by some North American churchmen as well as by some South American, but he felt that he had a charmed life, that he would escape bullets, that he could make his 'church' on any street corner, if he chose, and that he would find listeners and believers.

A slow revolution was sweeping the world, but unfortunately causing a great number of deaths. In the next many approaches or attacks of the peasantry, even in the Philippines, the peasants and workers were more numerous than they had been in the skirmish in Bogotá that had killed the Pope, because they had had time to assemble. The haciendas, factories, residential enclaves were prepared too with tear gas, fire hoses, tall steel gates, and machineguns, but the fact was, there were even more peasants and workers than bullets. In many battles, the workers rushed over the bodies of their fallen, entered houses and took them over. Then began 'confrontation', talking. The people were in the main calm, realising their number and their power, and they frequently cited the Church and God as being on their side.

There were brawls in Ireland, in Belfast and Londonderry, fistfights and minor riots in Manhattan, as people tried to take account of an unusual event that all knew to be an injustice: the assassination of a Pope who had spoken out for justice for humanity and the individual. The Pope had asked for 'Peace' in his last moments, and it seemed that humankind hated itself for striking the Pope down, for allowing his death to happen. But ostensibly, the riots and squabbles were over abortion versus the anti-abortionists, for instance, rather specific issues.

Only a very few wealthy men with private armies in South America and elsewhere won against the workers, physically speaking, and managed to smile and to tell one another verbally or by their attitudes that they had done 'the right thing' against 'militant Communists'. But the core of the revolution was in the core of the Catholic Church, and that was changed for ever. The workers might be back at work, but their conditions were better now, and the workers had a confidence that the landowners lacked. Of course, liberation theology priests and priests who had not mingled in such strife before had come out in such force and number, no state would have dared to try to shoot them, lock them up or even shut them up. European liberals were behind them, and so was the majority of the United Nations.

The reverberations of the two Red Slipper speeches went on for more than a year, like the after-rumbles of a volcanic eruption. Thousands lost their lives, many in truly peaceful street marches, which were misinterpreted by armed policemen and scared soldiers. Some said the toll of the dead was over two million. The Catholic Church had to yield on its anti-birth control and its anti-abortion stands, which it did in a passive way, by saying nothing when priests spoke out to their followers, and when the Pill and other means of contraception became easily obtainable in Ireland, for example. Doctors quietly began performing abortions, especially when both husband and wife desired one, and when word spread that local priests and bishops did not protest.

It was said and confirmed that attendance in Catholic churches increased markedly in America and France.

Now there was a new pope, John XXIV, elected just five days after the death of Sixtus VI. Pope John XXIV was keeping quiet, building his image still, after a year, as a tolerant but still devout Catholic. Meanwhile the usually rigid Vatican Curia and various bishops showed themselves capable of metaphysical and logical acrobatics and contortions, as they endeavoured to explain Sixtus VI's utterances as both interpretations of old and established dogma and aberrations of Pope Sixtus's thoughts, attributable to the Pope's exposure to heat in Mexico and Colombia and to an unusual swelling of his right great toe which gave him pain, a fact to which his physician Dr Franco Maggini could testify.

The 'red slipper fad' was just that, said *L'Osservatore Romano*, a fad which would die down, unworthy of the notice of dedicated men of God. Perhaps *L'Osservatore* wished it had not contributed even this much to red slipper publicity, because the fad did not die down, and little red slippers of all sizes proved themselves popular and decorative when a ring was fastened to them and they were worn around the neck, or as pins on women's blouses, or as tiny pins on men's lapels. Though revolutionary, the red slipper said, 'I am a believer still.'

PRESIDENT BUCK JONES RALLIES AND WAVES THE FLAG

Sunday was a devilish day at the White House, starting at 9 a.m. The President and the First Lady were in Washington, DC, which was exceptional, as Friday noon they usually took off via helicopter and jet to their Arizona spread, a big ranch called the Lucky Buck, and did not return until Monday afternoon.

This weekend, there had been a crisis, in fact two crises, one foreign and one domestic. In the past week, it had been discovered that the 'Administration' had been selling arms to both sides in a Middle East conflict, after having pledged not to sell to either side. The President had been assured that no one was going to blow this scenario, because *both* sides were benefiting, weren't they, and an awful lot of American arms dealers and middlemen were benefiting too. It could go on for ever, was the attitude of Buck's closest advisers, because that war between the two Gulf oil states had been going on for eight years now. Both sides held a few Americans as hostages, nearly fifty altogether, and it was hoped by Buck and his Administration that arms deliveries would soften the two countries up, make them more inclined to release their American prisoners. Then a member of Buck's own team, Fulton J. Phipps (known as Phippy), had blown it in what appeared to be an unpremeditated slip in a news interview. '. . . Since they're being supplied by us . . .' had been Phippy's phrase. What? Supplied what by us? Phippy had said, still blandly, 'Arms.' Fulton J. Phipps, forty-seven years old, had been a career government service man all his life, had been 'a close aide' to a couple of presidents in years past, had done some speech writing, knew everyone in Washington and was generally liked.

But now Phippy was sticking to his story, that America was now and had been supplying 'quite a lot of armaments' in the war between these two countries, whereas Buck and his pals had decided to say (and had) that only a few renegade arms suppliers had been selling to both sides or either side, that it had not been and was not government policy to do so. Phippy's gaffe, if gaffe it was, had been compared in the newspapers to Butterfield's in saying casually that Nixon's conversations with his staff on the Watergate matter were 'of course on tape'. After that remark, everyone had started clamouring to hear the tapes.

So the public wanted to hear more about the arms sales, because it appeared that the 'wrong side', or the more anti-American and extremist side in the Gulf war, was now winning because of the advantage of more U S A-made tanks than the other side had or had bought. This was the fanatical side that shouldn't win, in the opinion of most heads of state everywhere, certainly of Western European countries. In brief, in the past week the United States had made an ass and a liar of itself. The world was laughing, when it was not deploring and worrying about the future.

And little Millie Jones (she was diminutive compared to tall and burly Buck) had fairly blown her mind in the past days, trying to protect her husband. God knew she was loyal! 'Sack Phippy!' she had screamed within hearing of the White House servants, several journalists and members of Fulton J. Phipps's team, as it were, nice guys who liked Phippy and liked the President too.

Now it was Sunday morning, and Buck was still asking Millie the same question: had she held 'a little press conference' around 5:30 p.m. Saturday and repeated her anti-Phipps sentiments, or not? Millie wasn't saying, maybe, Buck thought, because she couldn't remember. But he hadn't lost his interest in trying to jog her memory. There was a lot else she might have said in the one- or two-minute talk that she might have had with reporters. The fact was, Millie often took a Scotch to sooth her nerves. This had even been hinted at in the press, and *in vino veritas* was often true even if the speaker forgets having said what was said. Consequently, the press loved to get Millie alone, even for half a minute. And Buck and the household staff and the secretaries always tried to steer Millie clear of the press, with their short, surprise questions that so often got answers.

The situation was especially painful to Buck Jones on that Sunday morning at exactly ten minutes to 11, when a White House limousine deposited him and Millie and two gorillas before the steps of a Presbyterian church, in time for 11 o'clock service. The theme this morning was 'What Can *You* Do for *God?*' according to a bulletin board outside.

'Head up!' Buck whispered. 'And *smile!*' He needn't have said the latter, because his wife's smile was stitched on. Face-liftings. He held her arm firmly under his, and nodded and smiled at a snapping press photographer.

'You're hurting my *hand!*' Millie said.

'Shush,' the President whispered. Millie might have staggered without his rigid arm under hers. Buck thought the press might comment on their closeness, saying they looked like newlyweds, which would be all to the good.

'If you want to know what I said yesterday,' Millie murmured into her narrow mink coat collar, 'I said – things wouldn't be *so* bad, if there hadn't been so many *elements* trying to cover up.'

'Elements?' the President whispered, alert.

'Well, okay, *people* – damn them! They're trying to cover up to protect *themselves.*'

'Well, isn't that normal?' Buck muttered, starting to focus his eyes and his famous smile on a church officer who was shaking the hands of people entering. '*Our* pleasure!' Buck said in response to whatever the official said, which he hadn't caught. 'Bless you!'

Was Millie teasing him, and hadn't said anything? The President couldn't concentrate on the sermon for thinking about this. Didn't matter, he didn't have to comment on the sermon to the preacher. He was thinking that Millie's off-the-record comments weren't always reported at once, but rather sprung a day or a week later, when it suited the press. They'd snidely insulted her three weeks ago, when she had given a somewhat befuddled speech before an audience in a Philadelphia college's indoor sports arena. She'd been half an hour late and had started reading the same page twice, until a female secretary had stepped up and turned the page. This had been attributed to over-zealousness in the anti-drug cause by one newspaper that had been shown to Buck, but Phippy – loyal and serious Phippy, twenty years Buck's junior – had said this might be sarcastic, and had told Buck that another paper had said that Millie simply preferred alcohol to drugs. A jocular columnist had already used this idea for a funny article. Buck boycotted this columnist, along with one cartoonist who was widely syndicated.

'Amen!'

They were out again, smiling, shaking a few hands.

Monday tomorrow, Buck was thinking. By this time tomorrow the Special Investigating Committee (SIC) would have been in session more than two hours. Their job was 'to get to the bottom' of how at least four hundred million dollars' worth of armaments, tanks and aeroplanes, and maybe more, could have got to two adjacent but opposing countries in the past year. The President was trying to confine it to a year, but it had been going on for three or four years. Phippy knew that too, Buck recalled, as Phippy was one of his old-timers from the beginning of his administration. Of course, half a dozen other top men knew too, but – and Buck had to admire them for this – they had so determined *not* to know about these arms sales, that they really didn't know. They hadn't simply forgotten, they'd never known, no, it was complete news to them. That was Buck Jones's idea of professional politicians, the kind of guys the country needed! And, for Pete's sake, look at the *money*! Armaments were made to be *sold* – and maybe used, too. So what were these Jesus Christs yelping about?

'Let me go!' Millie said at the limousine.

He'd been squeezing her hand too hard again. Buck came to, and gave her a kiss on the cheek.

A photographer or two snapped. Good.

After lunch, a couple of the President's closest aides, one a speechwriter and the other a secretary-right arm, came into the living-room with notes.

'These are the dates to remember, sir. You've seen them before, but if there's any question – if you'd like to look at them again – ' Richard Coombes, thirtyish, a small-town boy on the way up and Buck's secretary-right arm, smiled reassuringly at the President.

Buck glanced at the three-by-five cards, a size which went easily into a jacket pocket. The first card said: ONE, underlined in red, and below that, the first date of the first arms shipment that Buck knew of. About contents and price of first shipment, YOU DON'T KNOW BECAUSE YOU WEREN'T TOLD EXACTLY. Card TWO reminded him that his main source of information had been John B. Sprague, his Secretary of State. Sprague was the nearest Buck had on his staff to a Rock of Gibraltar. Sprague was one of the precious few who could look a man in the eye and deny knowing something that they did know. Sprague was probably lie-detector-proof.

'Okay,' said Buck, glancing at the rest.

'You're sure?'

'If I'm not certain, I'll call you back.' The fact was, Buck was getting sleepy. He liked a nap after lunch. He dismissed his speechwriter also, but as the two men were walking toward the door, the President said, 'I don't have to make a speech tomorrow, do I, Pete?'

Pete White, the speechwriter, turned. 'No, sir, but I wrote half a page, kind of good wishes and summing up for the end of the hearing tomorrow morning.'

'Later, maybe. Phippy's going to do most of the talking. Get on to Phippy.'

'I think he's well briefed, sir. Mr Sprague and I spent all morning with him.'

'Did you now! Good! Excellent!'

The President was soon asleep in houseshoes, pyjamas, a dressing gown, in a large easy chair, feet extended toward the fireplace. He had a dream about Communists. He pushed a button or two, and the power of America was unleashed by land, sea and air. Colourful bomb blasts lit up a tropical landscape somewhere in South or maybe Central America, and people got sizzled, blown to bits. All the Commies were killed, and the Americans emerged smiling, no one dead, no one smiling more broadly than himself – Buck – as he congratulated the American heroes on nationwide television and hung medals round their necks.

Buck woke up in cheerful mood. Sometimes his dreams of Communists were negative, the Commies were sour-faced, strong, resisted like a stone wall, and America lost. Buck always awakened in a foul mood from these 'losing' dreams.

As soon as Buck pressed a bell twice – a signal for coffee – things began to happen. Three phone calls awaited him: the first two were good-luck messages from a couple of Republican senators in regard to tomorrow's inquiry; the third was from an aide who said a choir intended to serenade, so could Buck have ready a few nice words for them? He offered the words: 'Gosh, I'm really surprised and honoured to have a whole choir on my doorstep on Sunday afternoon. Thank – '

'What choir?' Buck interrupted. 'From a church, y'mean?'

'From the church where you and Mrs Jones went today,' said the aide, whose name Buck had forgotten, though he knew the voice. 'We can't turn it off now. It'll last nine minutes about, and they'll come and leave by bus . . . Oh, in about half an hour.'

The President reluctantly got dressed in business suit, white shirt and a tie. Wouldn't do to be in slacks and sweater and shirt with open collar on this Sunday, when he was supposed to be working hard, mustering facts for tomorrow. It had taken the Attorney General (no pal of Buck's) three weeks to select a panel of twelve men for tomorrow's hearing. Buck had managed to get three replaced, but more he couldn't do, and the questions were going to be tough. Buck intended to stonewall it, with the aid of his three-by-five-inch cards, which held damn-all as to info and facts. 'Don't forget, Buck, Phippy's prepared to take the guff and the rap if it comes to that, so don't *you* worry,' one of his aides had said. That was true. Phippy had said to John Sprague, in Buck's presence, that he'd take the rap, because Phippy knew well that what they were doing was illegal. Well, Buck thought, not quite illegal, he shouldn't start thinking in those terms. But what they were doing was against declared policy of the land now, that those particular two countries weren't to get *any* armaments from the USA, because it was in the interests of world peace and the price of oil that their silly conflict stop as soon as possible.

'. . . *a present help* . . .' wafted through the closed windows of the President's bedroom, where he had just finished dressing. The choir had already arrived.

A servant knocked, and announced that the President was expected now on the front steps.

'Be strong, and ye shall inherit the . . .'

Dusk had fallen. At least fifty children ranging from ten to fifteen years of age had aligned themselves below the bottom step of the White House in three rows. They were singing a hymn without a musical instrument to accompany them, but with the guidance of a singing master who had his back turned to the President.

'Good! And just say, "That's not my *style* – not my name – not my style – not my *name* . . ."' This was Millie, standing and singing about three steps up from the choir and on the left from the President's view. She was singing, badly, her anti-drugs song 'Not Me!' which truly clashed with the hymn.

'Millie? – *Millie!*' cried Buck, descending. Millie evidently thought she was beholding a bunch of drug addicts or converts from drugs.

'You can all make it! You're *lovely*! You – '

Buck caught her hard by the arm. But he smiled. 'Millie? – Hi, folks!' He whispered in her ear, 'Millie, it's a *church* choir. This isn't – ' He had to stop, because he couldn't come out with 'a drug addict rally' when God knew what kind of mikes might be picking all this up. 'Be *stro-ong* . . .' Buck sang, joining in the second chorus.

The youthful group lifted its arms, grinning, after the final note, and at once Buck Jones responded gracefully:

'Thank you, one and all. Gosh, I'm really surprised and honoured to have a choir on my own doorstep on Sunday afternoon!'

'Yee-aye!' the kids roared back, laughing, and clapping in appreciation, though many wore gloves, as the air was nippy.

Then the President escorted Millie up the steps toward the White House door, and was joined by two gorillas who appeared from behind pillars. Still holding Millie's right arm rigid under his, he said through his grin, 'Smile. Raise your left arm to the kids!'

Millie did. But once inside the White House, she turned to Buck and said, 'You don't love me!' in a whiny, tear-laden voice.

'Oh, my God!' said Buck, smiting his forehead. They were now in the round lobby whose acoustics were superb, but Buck knew that the staff and the gorillas had already heard just about everything by now. And so had he from *them*, if he thought about it. Even without his hearing aid turned up to full reception, Buck had picked up remarks like, 'Goddam place is falling apart, I swear,' in a whisper. Or 'It's a sinking ship and the effing rats're leaving.' A few people had recently resigned, true.

'Tomorrow's going to be one tough day,' the President was saying a few minutes later to Richard Coombes in the privacy of the living-room again. Millie had gone to her own bedroom. 'Best if Millie's not here. What about arranging for her to visit that drug rehabilitation centre outside of Houston. What's its name?'

'The New Start Ranch,' Coombes said. 'But we used a rehabilitation centre the last time, sir. Lots of other possibilities like – Ah, there's a gardening show opening in Atlanta tomorrow. Winter greenhouses. The flowers'll look good on TV and Atlanta'll be pleased if we tell them Mrs Jones is coming.'

Buck smiled. 'What would I do without you, Dick? Try it. – Bet she'll go. If you have trouble, let me know. Tell her tomorrow's for the birds – closed session inquiries, I'm out for lunch, and plooped by five in the afternoon.' Still, Buck managed a laugh at this awful prospect.

'That's just what I wanted to go over again with you, sir. The picture is this. – Yes, let's both sit down. This whole thing is so enormous, this arms sale – '

'The *media's* blowing it up!'

'I meant – it's widespread and involves a lot of people, sir. So many, that I think it's safe to say a couple of these air carriers, never mind how many or even when, got hijacked, captured by fundamentalist nuts. I don't mean it's true, sir, but we'll say it. Arms and money're missing. Maybe some of these air shipments had been destined for Israel, so what, perfectly legal. If this has been going on five or six years, we – '

'Ten months.'

'That's what *you* say, sir, and what you believe *and* what you've been told.'

'In other words, I'm right,' said Buck with his most convincing look as he gazed at Dick Coombes.

'Yes, sir. You stick to that, that's fine. My point is about *reality*. Because those guys tomorrow are going to confront *you* with a couple of billion dollars' worth of stuff, not just millions, and a long period of time, and names galore, from Israel to Turkey to – '

'*Turkey?*'

'Well, never mind Turkey, he's just a guy *from* Turkey. Back to the point. This has been going on a long time by land, sea and air. The money – what there is left of it – has been going to fight Communism in Central America, true. You didn't know about that till a few days ago, that's what you're going to say tomorrow, because your staff – the ones connected with this – were going to save it as a *surprise* for you on your birthday next month, in March.'

'As I recall – recall,' said the President thoughtfully, 'the freedom fighters in Central America claim to've received just about twenty thousand bucks – in all.'

'First, they're lying, as usual. Second, their own leaders have pocketed God knows how much. We mustn't try to pin 'em down, sir.'

'Oh, no,' the President agreed.

'Back to tomorrow. You're bitterly sorry about the seventeen American hostages who were beheaded on television ten days ago. I *would* mention that, seriously, sir.'

'Oh, yes,' said Buck solemnly.

'I'll make a note to make a three-by-five card about that beheading. But our selling to both sides – which you have known a *little* about – was meant to make friends of *both* countries, you see. No use making a friend of one country and an enemy of the other, is there?'

'Agreed, Dick. And what the hell, look at the profit! It's led to more fighting, true, but that means more *arms* sales, doesn't it? What I can't understand is why some of these people're so hopping *mad*!'

'Because arms sales are forbidden without knowledge of Congress, sir.'

'Congress be damned! I had enough of them when I ordered the mining of – What harbour was that?'

'Yeah, but mining a harbour's an act of war, sir, same as war, and in the Constitution only Congress can declare war.'

Buck Jones shook his head, bored. 'Too complicated for me. Congress has too many people in it. They just sit there – while American hostages are taken and their heads cut off one week and their brains blown out the week before that, and Congress doesn't do a thing. We – I – *my* folks here in the White House at least tried.'

'But that's what you can't say tomorrow, sir. The arms sales weren't anything to *do* with hostages, because you'd pledged to stonewall it there. "No knuckling down to terrorists," you said, *we* said.'

The President nodded, letting it sink in.

Buck and Millie watched a film before bedtime, a tale of American derring-do in the Old West, with a hero who was his own man and took orders from no one. Millie sipped a rum and cola. Buck, in good mood after the film, was afraid to mention the Atlanta trip to Millie, lest she blow up and say she wasn't going. She did not like these little official junkets where she had to cut a ribbon, make a brief speech, smile at journalists and photographers. She preferred to be at home, supervising the polishing of her silverware collection (tea sets, sugar bowls, gifts from heads of state), and checking that the housemaids had done their waxing of the furniture, and conferring with her secretary Ethel on the maintenance and improvement of the public image of herself and Buck.

Still Buck had a hard time falling asleep, unusual for him. He was trying not to think about tomorrow – things always came out fine for him, always had, hadn't they? – but he couldn't get his mind away from the hearing, which was to begin at 10 a.m. He conjured up the nervous but optimistic face of Fulton J. Phipps, good old Phippy ever eager to serve, to help. Phippy would be ready with the answers tomorrow, in case the President faltered. No one had said that he was going to be questioned alone in a closed room. No, he'd have his loyal friends around him.

At last Buck slept. But when he was awakened by a buzzing beside his table lamp, it seemed to Buck that he had just dropped off. He picked up the house telephone.

'This is Dick Coombes, sir. Fulton Phipps's wife just telephoned me and – she's in a state. Phippy's dead, sir.'

'*What?* – What d'y' mean dead?'

'Overdose, sir. According to his wife. She noticed – Well, she's so shook up, she hasn't phoned a doctor yet or a hospital, just me, because she knows I can reach you any time and . . .'

Buck saw on his luminous dial clock that it was twenty past 5. *Suicide.* That didn't play. Buck's brain began to work intuitively, the way it worked best. 'Listen – ' he cut through Dick's stammerings. 'Phippy's got a swimming pool, hasn't he?' Phippy had a fine property in Fairfax just outside Washington, DC. Buck had been there a few times. 'You get that arranged so Phippy drowned himself accidentally. Got that, Dick?'

'But – It's February, sir, and nobody's swimming.'

'*Do* it! We can't have a suicide in this scenario!' Buck shouted, as if he were the hero of the film he'd seen a few hours ago. He hung up.

'Darling – '

Buck's loud voice had awakened Millie, despite her sleeping pill. Buck was putting on his dressing gown. 'Trouble at the ranch. Got things to do. Go back to sleep, Millie.'

'. . . time is it?'

Buck didn't bother answering. He was thinking. *Coffee, barrels of it*, he remembered as a line from a good film he had seen, when things had suddenly swung into action in a US army camp because of an enemy attack. Real American efficiency, tough fighting by tough marines had carried the day. That was the way it would be now.

With his first cup of coffee in the living-room where the fire still glowed, Buck was on the telephone with his Secretary of State John B. Sprague. 'Sorry to wake you at this hour, John, but something's happened.'

'Not another kidnapping – '

'Worse. Phippy's killed himself . . . Yes, I just heard from Dick Coombes, who heard it from Phippy's wife. Now look – we can't *have* this. It may be that we have to postpone the hearing this morning, for some reason, because I sure as hell am not going to face 'em without Phippy. You get me?'

Sprague did. Sprague was a bearish kind of man, slow and heavy, wordy when he talked, but the kind who could always keep his nose clean, consequently the noses of others clean too. 'Suicide,' he murmured as if pondering the fact.

'Which is going to be an *accident*. Now – you telephone the Attorney General, John. We've got to have an official statement – '

'Attorney General? Don't you mean – um-m – maybe a coroner, sir?'

'Y-yeah, you're right, sorry, I mean the guy who certifies – what's happened. This is going to be a drowning . . . Well, don't ask me to explain *now*, because I have to go see Phippy's wife and pronto. Just get the head coroner in Washington, whoever he is, and ask him to get to the Fulton Phipps house in Fairfax *now*. Tell him it's an emergency and the President's orders.' Then Buck tiptoed into the bedroom, where Millie had fallen back to sleep, got an address book and returned to the living-room. He dialled Phippy's private number. By now it was five minutes to 6.

'Hello?' said a female voice, shaky and tear-filled.

'This is Buck, Laura,' said Buck in a deep masculine voice, having just seen in the address book that Phippy's wife was named Laura. 'You haven't called the hospital yet?'

She gave a sob, a burst of pent up sorrow. 'I – Phippy's *dead*!'

'You're by yourself,' Buck continued with the same calm. 'Okay, we'll be there, dear. Don't you get overwrought. Make yourself some tea. We'll be there in – maybe fifteen minutes. – Is your swimming pool full?'

'Swimming pool? It – It's full but with the cover over it for winter. You know, to keep the leaves out? – Why're you asking about the pool?'

'See you very soon, Laura dear.'

Next was Coombes, who in fact had been waiting on another line to get through to the President. While the President was speaking with Dick Coombes, a servant knocked and entered, wanting to know if he was ready for his breakfast.

'Orange juice and a croissant, please, Tim. And more coffee.' Buck continued to Coombes, 'I heard from his wife that the pool's full but with a winter cover over it. So we'll remove the cover.'

'Well – sure, I understand, sir. But it's occurred to me, water's not going to go into the lungs, not in the same way, maybe not at all – once a person's dead.'

That rang a bell with Buck, he'd heard it somewhere, and the hitch galled him, as did a lot of other hitches lately, and he stood up, gripping the phone. 'Okay, we'll damn well *pump* it into the lungs if we have to! Via a tube! What're we paying the chief coroner *for*? He's got a job today and he'd better do it! You read me, Dick? – Can you pick me up in about ten minutes? Door of the West Wing.'

A powerful lever had occurred to the President. Mrs Fulton J. Phipps would not want it known that her husband was a suicide. There was something shameful about a suicide, something that implied that a man hadn't been able to face what he'd been supposed to face. Whereas, if her husband had died by drowning in his swimming pool, having an early morning dip before an important hearing, this suggested that he'd been in top form, exercising body and mind before his appointed tasks. Chilly morning, yes, Phippy had always been game, but this time a cramp must have caught him and finished him.

Millie awakened as Buck was tying his blue and yellow tie, and straightening it under the collar of a fresh white shirt. 'Why so early, Buck? – What's happening?' she asked sleepily.

'Phippy – ' Buck turned toward her, prepared for this. 'Phippy was taking a swim this morning in his pool and drowned. They're trying to bring him around, but I don't think it's going to work. So I'm going over to see – '

'Swimming? In this freezing weather?'

'Maybe they've got a heated pool, I don't know.'

Millie raised her head a little. 'Did you say he's *dead*?'

'Yes, honey! I swear! That's what I heard from his wife this morning. That's what woke me up.'

'Well, who's – That so-and-so! To kill himself *now*! Letting you down!'

Sometimes Millie's intuition was uncanny. 'Don't yell it for the whole house to hear! – I'm going to do what I can, call off the agenda today, if I can.'

Dick Coombes collected Buck Jones a few minutes later, Buck having declined to be accompanied or trailed by the usual pair or quartet of gorillas. They sped out of Washington in the thin traffic of early morning, and entered the plush residential area of Fairfax with

173

its handsome two-storey mansions nearly obscured by great oak and walnut trees that stood on well-kept lawns.

Unfortunately, a woman neighbour had joined Laura. Both women were in the kitchen when Buck and Dick arrived.

'Laura,' said Buck tenderly, recognising her, giving her a gentle embrace with one arm when she stood up. 'I'm really sorry.'

'He couldn't face it,' said Laura, looking at the President with reddened eyes. 'He knew he was supposed to lie this morning – as *much* as he could – to protect you. And he hated it!'

'What d'you mean lie?' the President asked. 'This silly business of selling arms to two countries – You'd think it was the crime of the century! It's Phippy who matters, who – '

'I'm sick of it!' Laura said.

'Mr President, Phippy wrote a suicide note. Would you like to see it?' asked the woman neighbour in a gentle voice.

'Don't show it to him, I won't have it!' said Laura.

'Try to be calm, please, ma'am,' said Dick Coombes soothingly.

At that moment, they all heard the knocker at the front door. The coroner had arrived, accompanied by a man with a kit such as doctors carry.

The President shook the coroner's hand. The coroner introduced himself as George Davies, and introduced the other man, Dr Munzie, there were murmured introductions all round, then they filed into the bedroom where Fulton J. Phipps lay on his back with the covers pulled up to his chin.

Buck Jones at once began his speech. 'Ladies and gentlemen – and especially you, Laura. We all know that suicide is a terrible thing, a shameful thing – in the eyes of most of the world, and especially in the eyes of the people of our great country. Consequently, both I and my closest advisers deem it appropriate that Phippy's death be attributed to drowning in his own swimming pool after taking an early morning nip – dip,' the President corrected himself, frowning with earnest thought.

The neighbour spoke up. 'Why, the pool's got its winter cover on it still! And the water's icy!'

'You have my orders,' said the President, looking at Coroner Davies. 'May I remind you that I am your commander-in-chief.'

'We are going to remove that pool cover now, ma'am,' said Dick Coombes to Mrs Phipps, in a firm voice that a hypnotist might have envied, or respected anyway.

Things began to move. The doctor and Dick Coombes went out of the back door and got to work on the pool cover. Leaves had to be raked out of a puddle in the centre of the cover first, then ropes untied from stakes that held the cover by rings around its edges. Beneath, the water looked reasonably clean and clear. They folded the canvas cover and got it out of sight in a tool shed near the house.

Within the house, the President had expressed his wishes to Coroner Davies: he was to certify that Phippy had died from drowning. Even Laura Phipps seemed by now to take the attitude 'What did it matter?' since her husband was dead, anyway. But her hostility toward the President was apparent.

'Can't you force water into the lungs?' asked Buck Jones in a soft voice, with a glance at the pale profile of Phippy just a couple of metres from where he stood.

'Why bother, sir?' replied Coroner Davies, looking not at all happy. 'If we say it – if I say it – that he died from drowning, and if Mrs Phipps agrees – '

'Be damned to the lot of you!' said Mrs Fulton Phipps.

'You'll be well recompensed, Laura,' the President intoned. 'Never fear – for the rest of your life – '

With something between a scream and a moan, she quit the room, heading for the kitchen.

' – no one's going to challenge us and perform an autopsy,' the coroner continued. He had just been promised a very handsome fee for his services today.

And so it was announced to the media by 9 that morning that Fulton J. Phipps had drowned in his Fairfax pool, just a couple of hours before he was to testify before the Special Investigating Committee on the selling of arms to the two opposing Gulf region countries at war with each other, and on possible embezzlement of huge sums by a party or parties unknown. Laura Phipps had to be hospitalised and put under sedation, which, it was assumed by Buck Jones and his aides, the public would consider normal. Before 9 a.m., Buck had told someone to inform the head of SIC that the hearing scheduled for that morning would have to be called off, because of the sudden death of Fulton J. Phipps, a key testifier, by drowning earlier that morning. 'Phippy had been keen to go and speak,' was a statement attributed to Mrs Phipps, the peppy tone of which implied that Phippy had been so on top of the world that morning that he had decided to take a swim.

By 12 noon, however, this disorderly but still understandable scenario had taken a sharp turn, or come into very sharp focus. Someone – maybe the neighbour of Laura Phipps, maybe even a joker, though jokes could not surpass reality in the Buck Jones Administration – said that Fulton J. Phipps, known as Phippy, had taken an overdose at home, that his wife had found him dead in bed very early Monday morning, that he had left a suicide note which his wife had not allowed anyone to see. And worse, the joke or the rumour went on, it was 'the Administration' that had stepped in at once and tried to attribute the death to drowning in an outdoor pool, when the temperature had been three degrees above freezing. Macabre and touching political cartoons were inspired by this story. But one thing was certain in everyone's mind: Fulton J. Phipps had had the choice of lying or of telling the truth, and plainly hadn't been able to face either prospect.

Television, radio and satellite had this dramatic story all over the world by noon and 1 p.m. Washington time. Another cover-up? Could it be that the Administration had somehow bumped Phippy off? In truth, there was not much left to cover up. Buck Jones and his aides, even John B. Sprague, the sturdy water buffalo, had all lied, some more than others, and knew more than they admitted knowing. That day on the air and on TV there were suggestions that Buck Jones was about to or ought to resign, that he was finished, that no one at home or abroad believed anything he said any more.

Millie Jones was most upset, though she took an attitude of holding the fort, the fort being the White House and its chief her husband. She had that morning learned about and asked her secretary Ethel to cancel the Atlanta date, with her regrets. At 10, having switched on the news while dressing and doing her make-up (with extra care), Millie heard a joke at the conclusion of a programme: the announcer had said that, though the Administration might have no recognisable foreign policy, it had a plain-as-day domestic policy, which was that the top men in Buck Jones's circle intended to hang on to their jobs and salary no matter what.

Millie's resentment of this 'joke' was not mitigated by the resignation of two members of the White House staff before noon, one in the economics department, the other in Buck's public relations department, on the grounds of having been offered 'more challenging jobs' elsewhere. Ethel informed Millie that Laura Phipps had elected to go home from hospital (she had not been under sedatives but merely observation), and perhaps it would be tactful if Millie visited her. Millie emphatically agreed, and spent nearly an hour on the telephone, with the aid of Ethel, trying to persuade Laura to allow Millie to come and see her at her Fairfax house. But Laura was adamant, and wanted to be 'at home with a friend or two, thank you'. At half past noon, Millie tried to reach Buck by intercom to have lunch with him, but a male voice Millie did not recognise said that the President was going to lunch alone with his new spokesman Vince Donegan.

'New spokesman? What about Chet?' Yes, where had Chet been yesterday or this noon, when the news of Phippy had broken?

'Chet Swanson says he's overtired, ma'am, and can't do a good job any more. Those're his words . . .'

Millie didn't bother asking whom she was speaking with. She wished she could be with Buck at lunch, as he briefed the new man on an important job, but she also knew that when Buck was as tense as he was now it might be best without her.

She had a comforting glass of Scotch on the rocks before a lunch of cold roast beef and cottage cheese. Millie had invited Ethel to join her. They turned on the radio news as well as a couple of TV sets in the room where they lunched, and Millie was riled by a statement from the Russian premier. ' "The ball is now in Mr Jones's court," the Russian leader said on announcing that he had halted all nuclear tests until further notice, and he repeated his offer to reduce by a flat ten percent the number of nuclear warheads at present in the Russian arsenal, if the United States is willing to match this . . .'

'He's lying, I don't believe a word of it,' said Millie, as if to herself, staring at the TV set.

'There has been an unusually large explosion caused by a bomb or bombs dropped on a Gulf port. This news is *just* coming in,' the radio announcer went on in a taut voice. 'According to eye witnesses, the blast lit up the sky like a hundred suns and is still burning. There are rumours that it may have been an atom bomb, but this has by no means been confirmed – as yet. Rumours are said to be circulating as to whether Russia, because of its animosity toward . . .'

'Damn them,' said Millie. She had finished her lunch, having hardly touched her food, and her plans were made. Millie dismissed

Ethel before dessert and coffee, and retired to her quarters for fortification in the form of a soothing nip of Scotch in her locked bathroom. Whatever people said, alcohol did both soothe the nerves and give a lift. The important thing was not to overdo it, of course. The number of people even *she* knew, who simply weren't able to function without nearly a bottle a day – Well! Yet where would the world be without them? Buck hardly drank anything, and look at him now! Misjudgements right, left and centre. Buck hadn't used to be so, Millie thought. Lately, he was too trusting of people, took it for granted everybody loved him, loved *him*. Well, maybe they did, but they were out for themselves first and Buck Jones second. Millie set her empty Scotch glass down firmly, checked her short, fluffed hairdo in the looking-glass, and went out.

She went directly to the President's office, which she knew was empty now, because Buck was still out to lunch. She opened the door of a room off this, a smaller room with a desk and a couple of chairs, and stood looking at a small keyboard set atop the desk. It had fifteen or twenty buttons. Millie pressed the upper right to put the board in operation. The key word for what she wanted was 'Replay', though this scenario had never been played live. She pressed Replay, which nestled upper left among other buttons named Litex, Tryon and such. Three, two, one were next, she recalled, and pressed these. A green light appeared on one button. Millie was pleased with herself for having remembered so well, and for now *doing* something for her husband and for her country.

Sani was the last button she pressed, which might as well mean 'Fire!' Sani was Frankfurt, and this meant an order to fire a first nuclear warhead at a certain military base and munitions depot within the USSR. It was considered a 'warning' compared to what the USA could do, Millie remembered Secretary of Defence Somebody telling Buck. She had not been present when someone had gone through the button-pressing with Buck, but Buck had later taken her into this office, and with great pride and the current off showed her how it worked. She had written down the procedure a few minutes later, or maybe even there on the spot, she couldn't remember, considering doing so a safety measure against a bumbling fool pushing them at some time, or even Buck in an angry or overconfident moment: she'd at least know what someone was doing if she saw it. But now, the time had been ripe, just perfect, Millie felt. Russia would cower. The world would see that the USA wasn't paralysed by silly domestic problems, and wasn't going to take lying down Russia's dropping of a nuclear missile smack on to a Gulf port – so vital for *oil* to the USA and Western Europe!

Frankfurt's American Forces Nuclear Readiness station fired their missile within twelve minutes of Millie's button-pressing, and this over the head of a colonel who argued in vain that they ought to radio back for confirmation. The general in command wanted to fire.

Russia's military base and the munitions there exploded, killing a couple of hundred soldiers and a few civilians at once, sending nearby towns into panic: people fled, shielding their eyes from the fearful blast in the sky which up to now they had merely seen pictures of. Fires broke out in entire villages, though this military base was considered to be in 'a thinly populated area'. Moscow was not slow in reacting. A big military plane was dispatched bearing a dummy or drone plane in the direction of the American eastern coast. At the right moment, the mother plane would release the drone, which was programmed to head for Philadelphia.

A top-level American general and also an admiral were trying to reach the President: was this nuclear bomb report from Frankfurt an accident? Or had war been declared?

The President, after a long and informal talk with his new spokesman Vince Donegan, had decided to take Vince to meet Laura Phipps, which would be an exercise in diplomacy and finesse for Vince.

'Keep talking – look her in the eye,' said Buck as the chauffeur-driven car slid up to the Phipps house in Fairfax. The President carried flowers. At that moment, the intercom in the President's limousine sounded, and the URGENT button turned red. Buck picked up the telephone, and said, 'Yes?'

'Frankfurt has just dropped a nuclear warhead on Russian soil, sir . . . Yes, *our* forces, sir, on orders.'

Buck was just taking this in, looking at the equally shocked and blank face of Vince Donegan, who had heard the voice, when a woman poked her face close to the half-open window on the President's side.

'You'd better leave, Mr Jones.' It was the woman friend of Laura Phipps, whom Buck Jones had seen earlier that morning, and she looked grim. 'Laura heard the news report about Phippy – saying it was a swimming pool accident. She's disgusted and she's going to tell the truth! So – scat, Mr President!' Her eyes flashed.

Buck had the feeling that a wild tiger was near, about to strike. 'Joey – get going! Back to the – back home, please,' Buck said to his driver.

Marines were deploying themselves round the White House when Buck and Vince rolled up the driveway. A gorilla who opened the car door said, 'Important news, sir, you're to go into your office right away.'

The news was that Moscow had launched an aircraft with a drone carrying a nuclear warhead, which the Russians offered to call off, on word from Washington that the Frankfurt firing was an accident.

'Frankfurt *firing*?' asked Buck. 'But who ordered this firing? – Dick! Boy, am I glad to see you!' The President smiled.

Dick Coombes had just trotted up, in shirtsleeves and with his tie loosened. 'C-come into my office, sir.'

The atmosphere in the big lobby where Buck had just stood had been tense with fear, even unfriendliness, Buck had felt. Four or five men whom he knew well had been standing speechless, looking at him. 'That Russian missile's on the *way*?' Buck asked when Dick had closed the door of his office.

'Millie pressed the Replay system. Around one o'clock today or just after, sir. It went to Frankfurt and Frankfurt obeyed orders. Now what we – '

'Judas K. Priest! Is Millie out of her mind?' Buck turned toward the door. 'Where the hell is she?'

'Sir! We're pressed for *time*! Our best bet – and I've had time to check with a couple of generals – is to say this was a technical error, human error, what the hell, but an *error*. And please to call off the plane with the *drone*. That's what we ought to say to the Russians.'

'I don't say "please" to the Russians,' replied Buck Jones, setting his jaw.

'The Russians – ' Dick Coombes said with a scared sigh, 'said that missile is headed for the Philadelphia area. That'll affect New York – maybe us here.'

'We'll intercept it. What're our interceptors for? Let's test 'em out on something real. Was that Russian plane picked up on satellite? Are they tracking it?'

'By satellite, yes, sir, but it's flying very high now, and to *hit* it –

That's like continuing the war, if you see what I mean. Consider for a minute, sir. Best to say the Frankfurt bomb was – '

A strange moan interrupted Dick Coombes, deep, eerie, penetrating. He didn't know what it was, but the President did.

'That's the White House bomb alert. Atom bomb,' said Buck. 'Jumping the gun a little, maybe. That Russian plane's barely past France by now.'

Dick Coombes gulped. 'They're probably taking the Pole, sir, coming in from north-east. Maintenance said they were going to test the alarm.'

Doors opened. Bells rang, bells on Dick's desk.

Generals were demanding on telephones: Who was in charge? No one could find out for the next forty-five minutes, or even after that. The news of the Russian atom bomb being on its way had reached the media nationwide, and the East Coast in particular was in a state of disorder and panic.

Buck Jones asked for a minute's time on radio and TV, but his secretary reported back that no radio or TV crew could get to the White House, as local traffic police had declared a state of emergency, mainly for White House protection.

'Okay, give 'em a message – from me,' Buck said. 'We'll smash this bomb coming. We'll smash it right out of the sky. Got that?'

Buck was told that Millie was in her own office, so Buck headed for his wife's suite, which consisted of ante-room, office, and a bedroom. She was with her secretary Ethel, dictating something, when Buck knocked and was admitted.

'*Yes*, I sent the Replay message to Frankfurt,' said Millie. 'It's time this Administration recovered its dignity and authority – and this is the way to do it!'

Millie was high as a kite, Buck saw, but he was so uptight himself that some of her confidence invaded him, made him feel slightly better. 'Well, Frankfurt sure as hell obeyed,' Buck said. 'But listen, honey, we could – *still* could tell the Russians that Frankfurt was a technical error. Then they'd call off *their* bomb. One's coming. Did you know that? Atom bomb heading for Philly?'

'Yes, someone told me. That's to be expected. Send up a detonator when it's near enough. Meanwhile, *we* need to send off one or two more. I was leaving that to you, Buck.' Millie's tense smile widened slightly. She sat upright on her sofa, erect as a horseback rider. 'You go in there and do it.'

Buck knew she meant the control room off his study. He nodded, acknowledged the silent Ethel with the slightest of nods, and turned on his heel. 'All signals go,' he said over his shoulder.

Send one off from Munich, Buck Jones was saying two minutes later on a private telephone in the little room off his office. His voice sounded odd in his own ears on this telephone. *Oh, you guys figure that one out,* Buck said cheerfully, in reply to the question *What targets are we supposed to hit?* from a general to whom Buck was talking.

By now it was after 3 p.m. Satellite data predicted that the Russian bomb would strike Philadelphia around 7 p.m.

'Unless you call this off, sir,' said Dick Coombes. 'The Russians haven't released that drone yet.'

John B. Sprague was standing in a corner of the President's study just then, silent, head bent, though his gaze was fixed on Buck Jones.

'That'd be backing down, wouldn't it?' asked Buck, grinning. 'We're not backing down. We've got an *arsenal.*'

'So've the Russians,' said Sprague. 'Come on, Buck, want to think for a minute? Half a minute?' Sprague's bear-like figure in a tweed suit came forward a step or two and he wagged a finger. 'We've got two or three hours at most, Buck – but I wouldn't count even on that much – to call this game off. We'd call our bombs off too, of course.'

'What's this, you being gun-shy, John? Running scared? You think we're not a match for the Russkies?'

There were a few more exchanges between Buck and the other two, but essentially Dick Coombes and John B. Sprague gave up in regard to persuading the President. There came a time when Buck Jones simply wasn't listening any more.

'A friend of Phippy's wife told me to scat today,' Buck added for good measure. 'I ain't scatting.'

So the bombs soared on, and Washington, DC and the USA prepared to take cover, if there was any. And so did Russia. Meanwhile, Europe, the fly-over territory, beseeched both super-powers to call the whole thing off, and hoped that a bomb wouldn't fall short and hit their own territory, England, France, or whatever.

But even at 4 and 5 o'clock Eastern Standard Time, there were doubts, questions in New York and elsewhere. Were the bombs for real, or were both the USA and USSR threatening, seeing what the other side would do, or say? The President had not made a statement as yet about firing an atom bomb, and neither had Secretary of State Sprague. The stories of flying bombs were merely leaks via the journalists who hung around the White House's front steps, asking questions of anybody and everybody.

By 5:30 p.m., a nervous Pete White, speechwriter, reached the President in the latter's study, and presented him with a statement of a hundred and fifty words typewritten. 'It's an announcement of the oncoming Russian bomb or bombs, sir. The public doesn't yet know whether to believe it – you see.'

The President was with Dick Coombes and a heavyish man in a general's uniform, looking at a big map spread before them on a table. The whisky bottle was out, and the general had a glass in hand. 'I realise,' said Buck, accepting the page from Pete White. 'But to have told people earlier would only have caused panic. Now's the time, I agree, on the six o'clock news, live. That gives people about an hour to –'

'But excuse me, sir, there's panic already! The highways are really clogged! – I'll arrange right away for the TV and radio crews –' Pete White wet his lips. His voice was hoarse.

'They should be heading for air-raid shelters,' Buck said. 'Millions of shelters, all over the country!'

Pete White winced, and exchanged a glance with Dick Coombes.

'There may well not be enough shelters, Buck,' said Dick.

The general looked bored with the conversation, and as if he wanted to get back to the map before him.

As the President opened his mouth to reply to Dick, the ominous moan sounded, the bomb alert.

'That's really *it* now!' said Pete White, raising his voice in order to be heard. 'The bomb's maybe close!'

'I intend to make that announcement. It's an *historic* announcement,' said Buck in the deep authoritative tone he could muster instantly, if need be. 'Get those media guys here, Pete. You too, Dick! – Sorry, General –'

'Wyman.'

'Wyman. Sorry, but first things first. I'll make the announcement, then we'll get back to where we bomb the Russkies.'

President Buck Jones insisted on speaking from the steps of the White House, which made it difficult for the TV crew (only one had been able to arrive) to set up its lights. A dozen mikes were poked toward the President as he intoned:

'Today – this historic day in February – circumstances have compelled the United States of America to hit back against what we perceive as a nuclear attack by Russia upon our interests – thousands of miles away in the Gulf region. It was with the deepest regret that we gave orders for a similar bomb to be launched from our Nuclear Readiness base near Frankfurt, Germany. Now – as we might have foreseen and did foresee – our enemy has chosen to launch a bomb of its own toward our sacred soil. This solemn message is to announce the cause of this peril, and to advise all citizens on the East Coast to leave their houses and apartments and head for their nearest air-raid shelter, and – failing a shelter – to close themselves in their cellars, taking with them water and some dry provisions such as beans, rice and powdered milk. America will win, because her cause is just. God bless you all and keep you.'

This was dramatic timing, as five seconds later the American public who had heard the speech (confirming their worst fears) had barely had time to say, 'Whew!' when the bomb fell, not exactly in the centre of sprawling Philadelphia, but near enough. The drone had been the target of some ground-to-air missiles fired from a couple of US navy vessels near the coast, but the missiles had missed.

Thousands of people were killed, scorched, blinded in seconds in Philadelphia. Several million others in creeping motor vehicles closed their windows and huddled, terrified, and kept moving south-west and north-west away from the burning, radioactive metropolis. In other regions of the East Coast, people clamoured and banged in vain at the closed doors of a few air-raid shelters and of farmers' cellars and the cellars of country houses everywhere. The air-raid shelters were in mountainsides or sometimes in farmers' fields, but there were more people than shelters, and in angry resentment some people pushed stones against the doors of shelters and even cellars, hoping the people inside would never emerge. The roads leading out of Philadelphia and New York were bestrewn with abandoned cars that had run out of gas.

That wasn't all, of course, the one bomb on Philadelphia. Others now fell on Chicago, San Francisco, and the middle of Texas. This was because the USSR had by 8 p.m. that evening Eastern Standard Time suffered hits from Munich and elsewhere, or at least was aware, thanks to satellite, of high-flying aeroplanes carrying bombs toward their land, and of long-range cruise missiles coming their way. Any calmness or tit-for-tat had vanished. Neither side was holding back, though both sides intended to save a proportion of their huge arsenals for a last ditch stand, if such a term could be used when the atmosphere would have become insufferable for animal and plant life.

Buck and Millie Jones had fled the White House by 6:45 p.m. leaving the servants to stow valuables into the White House basement, itself feared not to be a good shelter for the President and his wife, because the enemy attack was fiercest on the East Coast. The Joneses intended to go farther west. The helicopter pad of the White House had been by then overrun by White House staff with belongings, all awaiting chauffeur-driven cars or their wives in cars to pick them up, so the President's limo with driver and one gorilla headed straight for Dulles Airport.

A motorcycle escort cleared the way, edging private cars on to the shoulder if necessary, so that the President's car could pass others on the rather long drive to the airport. One would have thought all Washington, D C was leaving and heading for Dulles. There was still rougher behaviour at the airport, where fighting-mad people tried to get aboard aircraft of any kind. The gorilla pulled his gun, yelled, and charged toward Air Force One, whose position he knew thanks to his walkie-talkie.

The President's party took off, with Cincinnati, Ohio as its destination, a name that sounded inland and cosy to Buck and Millie by now. Millie had in her purse a full (nearly) flask of whisky, but a letdown had begun to set in. Scared and determined, she kept assuring Buck that she and he, *they*, had done the right thing. Some fresh oxygen was released by a thoughtful steward, and another steward brought them a meal of *filets mignons*.

'We might've thought of asking Laura Phipps to come with us,' Buck said to Millie. 'This is going to look bad in the press.'

'Wha-at? When Laura or her neighbour friend told you to get off her land? Let her sizzle!' Millie tackled her second *filet*.

At Cincinnati, they were unable to land, circled for half an hour, then radioed that they were running out of fuel (almost true), and repeated that the President and his wife were aboard, so a way was given, a rough landing accomplished. Everyone was leaving Cincinnati too, it appeared. People were afraid of fall-out, and heading west. On the other hand, a bomb by now had hit San Francisco, so why should anyone go west?

Well, there was Nevada, places like that, not so populated.

The President and Millie stood in the noisy terminal, Millie a bit miffed at the lack of reception for them.

'Let's get to a shelter – or whatever we're supposed to do for *safety*!' Millie yelled. 'Who's in charge here?'

'*I* am!' said Buck. 'Hey, Sam!' he called to the gorilla. 'Get in touch with Dick *Coombes*, would you?'

'At – Where is he, sir?' asked Sam.

The President tried to think, couldn't. 'Can't we radio him from Air Force One?'

Sam grimaced. 'I wouldn't want to try to get back to that plane, sir! There's a mob out there, all over the tarmac!'

'Get us a limo!' Buck said. 'You've got a gun!'

Sam again pulled his gun from its shoulder holster, and made a path for them toward a door marked TAXIS–BUSES. Still using the gun, the gorilla persuaded a taxi driver (who said he was heading for home) to take them. Sam told the driver to go to the nearest air-raid shelter.

'*Air-raid* shelter!' said the driver. 'There's one a few miles from here, but it's jam full and closed, I can tell you, because I took a couple of fares there. Just forget it.'

'Any others?' asked Sam.

The driver said he didn't know of any, so Sam and Buck agreed to try the jammed shelter and to force their way in, if necessary.

'Wouldn't a hotel be a lot more comfortable, Buck?' asked Millie.

'We can't take any chances,' Buck said. 'This is an emergency.'

The taxi made slow progress, going against airport-bound traffic which was spilling into the wrong lane. Then the driver had to stop for gas.

'Can't sell you more than one gallon,' said the station attendant. 'They say a bomb's coming this way and we've got to be fair to everybody.'

'Got the President of the United States in the back seat,' said the gorilla who had got out of the taxi.

'Oh, yeah? The guy who fired back – ?' The attendant, a man of about thirty who looked exhausted, hung up his gasoline nozzle and stared into the taxi's window. 'You're gettin' a gallon like anybody else. Damn you for firing – '

'We fired *back*!' cried Millie through a slightly opened window. '*Russia* fired – '

'Wasn't Russia! That's what the news said. It was some other country with a bomb that *we* let 'em have. Ain't got the time to argue, my wife's having a baby in the city hospital, or I wouldn't be here. You'll get your gallon and you can go to hell!'

'You don't talk like that to the President!' said the gorilla Sam, jutting his jaw. Besides being broad, he towered several inches over the station attendant.

'I don't give a you-know-what!' replied the attendant, nozzle in hand again. 'I'll give you and the President this gallon in the face, if you'd prefer it!' He yanked the tank cap off, and angrily started to release gas, eye on the meter behind him. 'Never mind paying, stuff your money.'

A mile or so farther on, they passed a closed diner. They were all thirsty for plain water. It was nearly 3 in the morning when they reached the air-raid shelter in a farmer's field on the left side of the road. It was merely a slight rise of land, easily missable, except that now several bonfires burned near it, and people sat round the fires huddled in blankets, like Indians.

'They ain't gonna open the doors,' one squatting-on-heels man said to Sam. 'No, sir, not even for the President, 'cause they full up in there!'

'Specially not for the President!' somebody said.

Others laughed. Whisky seemed to be flowing.

Sam clenched his fists and tried banging, shouting at the two closed doors, which slanted into the earth. The metal doors resembled those of a bank vault. He got no answer from them, and he gave up.

'Try the spot down the road!' a young male voice cried, and this was followed by shrieks of female laughter, guffaws from the men.

'What spot?' asked Sam.

'Thataway 'bout a mile and a half. Right side o' the road,' another voice said. 'But it's a *nuclear* shelter! Hah!'

'Yee-hoo-*hee*!' Maniacal laughter now from all round.

Sam was doubtful, but told the driver to go on in the direction they had been going, which was the way the bonfire people had pointed. This 'spot' was visible, thanks to a couple of lanterns on posts. Here some fifty or sixty people milled about, tending bonfires, while others appeared to be digging into the side of a hill with shovels and pickaxes. The President was by now asleep with his head in Millie's lap. Sam got out, tired, thirsty and hungry, but still in better shape than the taxi driver, who had collapsed now over the steering wheel. Dots of light, aircraft of all sizes, crept across the black sky, heading generally westward.

'You got a pick or a shovel?' was the question that greeted Sam.

'No. Is this an air-raid shelter?'

'Hah! Man, this is supposed to be, but this is a nuclear *waste disposal* shelter!'

'So the joke's on *us*, see?' said a slurry female voice.

'Then why're you digging here? You people making a cave?' asked Sam, seeking to ingratiate himself, because these people had food and drink. 'We can help, maybe.'

'We're digging because the ground is sort of loose, but all we run into is steel boxes, cement walls – '

'And maybe radioactivity,' said a girl's voice.

'But maybe less activity than what's gonna *hit* us!' said a male voice, and this was rewarded with loud laughter, sounding a bit drunken.

Sam hesitated, then said, 'Can you spare any water? Maybe a cupful? We're a party of four and we've been – '

'Buddy, we can't, so piss off!' A red-headed fellow, only the top half of him visible in a flashlight's beam, came forward. He was young and angry. 'You coming by taxi and asking *us* for water? This is our site. Only diggers allowed.'

'Scat! . . . Get lost! . . . We don't need no more!'

A rock the size of a baseball hit Sam in the chest, so he turned and walked as fast as possible in the darkness back to the taxi.

'Hey, *look*! That's *it*, ain't it?'

The excitement in the voice behind Sam made him stop and turn, and he saw it at once, a glow like a silvery moonrise, with a shaft of denser light going straight up its centre. Sam ran toward the taxi now.

Buck Jones had his elbow out of the window, grinning. 'Isn't it a beaut, honey?' he said to Millie. 'Look at it spread! We'll show 'em!'

'But that's *theirs*, not ours, Buck!' said Millie.

'No go here!' said Sam, awakening the driver with a poke in the shoulder. 'Let's move on!'

They got back into the traffic, the creeping stream of angry vehicles, passed another closed and dark roadside restaurant. And then they ran out of gas, the car gasped for a few yards, and stopped. Cars from behind bumped them, awakening the President who had fallen asleep again. Now Millie was sound asleep. Buck Jones asked the taxi driver to try the radio for news, and the driver did so. They were actually moving a bit now, being pushed by the cars behind them and beside them, but drivers behind them were shouting for them to get off the road.

'Radio's dead, mister,' said the taxi driver, and at that instant a heavy vehicle bumped the cab's left side, the taxi slid into a ditch and fell on its own right side. The highway was without illumination, and three cars followed the taxi into the ditch one after the other. The President and party were buried under the first vehicle and a half, meaning nearly two tons of steel and hysterical humanity, and it was a slow and painful, bloody and gasping death they had.

Before the dawn came, the sky over America and the whole temperate zone of the Northern Hemisphere had turned a pale purple in which clouds of silvery hue rolled and played, rose and sank. The colourful atmosphere – lethal – had its beauty as it seeped into the Southern Hemisphere in long slow streaks, causing millions to flee from it toward the South Pole. Now trusty little satellites still orbited the earth or stayed in place, as if nothing had happened, kept taking photographs and sending them earthward, where no one was alive or in a condition to receive them, except a few lonely army stations in the South Pacific. Artists had depicted such scenes in the past, Hieronymus Bosch, Max Ernst, Tanguy to some extent.

The people of the Southern Hemisphere when not fleeing gathered in groups small and large (several hundreds of people), attempted to share food equally, made speeches about the necessity of having hope and courage (the Church did well here), which sounded quite good, even though ninety percent of the speakers, formal and informal, did not believe a word of what they were saying. The rotating Earth had become entirely too saturated by radioactive atmosphere, which its gravitational force held fast. There seemed less wind or winds than normal, the last curse of all.